make me I'm yours...

# Just For Fun

D&C

David and Charles

www.rucraft.co.uk

## A DAVID & CHARLES BOOK

© F&W Media International, LTD 2011

David & Charles is an imprint of F&W Media International, LTD

Brunel House, Forde Close, Newton Abbot, TQ12 4PU, UK

F&W Media International, LTD is a subsidiary of F+W Media Inc.

4700 East Galbraith Road, Cincinnati, OH 45236

First published in the UK and USA in 2011

Text and designs © Sally Southern, Margot Potter, Jill Gorski, Claire Crompton, Julie Collings, Jenny Hill, Jenn Docherty, Sharon Bennett, Marion Elliot, Debbie Chialtas, Dorothy Wood, Julie Hickey and Louise Butt 2011

Photography and illustrations © F&W Media International, LTD 2011

ISBN-13: 978-1-4463-0069-5 hardback
ISBN-10: 1-4463-0069-2 hardback

Printed in China by RR Donnelley for F&W Media International, LTD Brunel House, Forde Close, Newton Abbot, TQ12 4PU, UK

10 9 8 7 6 5 4 3 2 1

**Publisher** Alison Myer
**Senior Acquisitions Editor** Freya Dangerfield
**Desk Editor** Jeni Hennah
**Project Editor** Lin Clements
**Proofreader** Cheryl Brown
**Design Manager** Sarah Clark
**Designer** Marieclare Mayne
**Photographers** Ginette Chapman, Christine Polomsky, Tim Grondin, Hal Barkin, David Peterson, Kim Sayer, Karl Adamson, Lorna Yabsley, John Carrico, Adam Leigh-Manuell, Adam Henry, Paul Barker, Ric Deliantoni, Simon Whitmore
**Senior Production Controller** Kelly Smith

F+W Media Inc. publishes high quality books on a wide range of subjects. For more great book ideas visit: www.rucraft.co.uk

# contents

Introduction     4

## Awesome Accessories
Felt Flower Necklace     8
Pretty Paper Earrings     12
Button Bangle     14
Jeans Bag     16
Magic Mitten Gloves     20
Simple Socks     26
Ballerina Slippers     30

## Groovy Gifts
Fabric Frames     36
iPod Sweater     40
Dishy Delight     44
Pucker-Up Purse     46
Birdie Album     50
Retro Cards     54
Cake Slice     56

## Tempting Treats
Stuffed Chicks     62
Neapolitan Soap Pops     66
Birthday Bunting     70
Button Baby Dolls     72
Funky Flowers     74
Cupcake Bag     78

## Techniques
Basic Tools     84
Preparing for Work     85
Sewing Techniques     86
Knitting Techniques     96
Crochet Techniques     108
Papercraft Techniques     110

Templates     114
Designer Credits     120
Index     121

# introduction

There are so many wonderful crafts today that it's hard to choose just one to focus on, but with this book you have an instant collection of bright and modern projects to create, from bags to bangles and socks to soaps. The twenty colourful and varied projects give you a taster of some exciting crafts, including sewing, knitting, papercraft, needle felting and soap making.

You'll have great fun working with fabulous fabrics, colourful papers, wonderful wools, beautiful beads and brilliant buttons, and along the way create fabulous treats for yourself or to give as gifts to family and friends.

All of the projects have been chosen with beginners in mind and each one is rated to give you an idea of how easy it is:

 Simplest of all, these projects take little more than assembling the lovely materials you have gathered together.

 Simple projects to start you off on discovering the great crafts featured.

 Easing you in, these projects round out your skills as you explore the fun new ways of spending your time creatively.

Whether you need an accessory to glam up an outfit, a funky gift for a friend or a trendy treat for yourself, you'll find what you need here. So pick a project and start having fun!

# awesome accessories

# felt flower necklace

Felt is such a great fabric to work with as it's easy to cut into shapes and doesn't fray. It's also available in a wide range of colours, which means you can choose shades that complement your favourite outfit. The necklace is quickly made using ready-made felt beads and a hand-sewn flower. A matching ring in jazzy colours is easily created to coordinate with the necklace.

The necklace design uses felt beads in different sizes and shapes, some decorated with beads and sequins for sparkle. A splash of brighter colour among the blues, such as a fresh lime, brings extra zing.

### you will need ...

* ❀ felt beads in complementary colours
* ❀ felt in turquoise and lime
* ❀ iridescent sequins and seed beads
* ❀ embroidery cotton (floss) in pale turquoise and mid blue
* ❀ selection of mid-sized glass beads in blues and greens
* ❀ a necklace fastening

**1** Make a flower, using the templates to cut a large flower out of felt and then a smaller flower out of lighter coloured felt in a similar tone. Using one strand of embroidery cotton in a matching colour sew tiny running stitches around the edge of each flower.

**2** Place the smaller flower on top of the larger one and sew together with a small felt bead at the centre. Decorate the felt bead with a sequin and random seed beads.

**3** Select the felt beads you want to use for the necklace and lay them out in order. Position the flower amongst the felt beads. Space out all of the beads and add a smaller glass bead in between each felt bead. Decorate some felt beads with seed beads or sequins, leaving others plain.

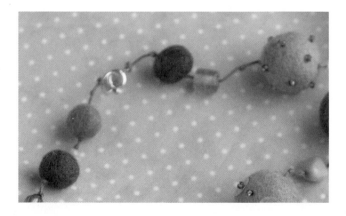

**4** Thread the beads together using three strands of embroidery cotton. Space the beads out by tying knots in the thread above and below each bead to keep it in place. Catch stitch the flower on to the embroidery cotton to hold it in place. Finish by stitching a jump ring and clasp on to each end of the necklace to fasten.

The embroidery cotton needs to be about three times the finished length of the necklace. Make sure it's long enough before you knot the beads.

Diamonds may be a girl's best friend but this eye-catching felt ring really has the wow factor and it can be made up quickly using the same technique as the necklace. For a ring you will need a felt bead, some felt for the flower, seed beads, embroidery cotton to match your felt, some strong glue and a ring base. Choose a ring base with a large area to glue the flower on to so that it holds in place securely. Use the templates to cut a large and small flower. Decorate the felt and make the flower as for the necklace. Glue the finished flower on to a ring base.

*techniques* basic tools... preparing for work... sewing techniques... attaching beads... templates

# pretty paper earrings

Make fab beads in a flash using resin stickers with pretty paper sandwiched in between. You can use any sort of paper – try newspapers, comics, magazines or stamped images. The possibilities are endless, so get creative!

## you will need ...

- ✿ clear resin stickers, two medium and two extra large
- ✿ handmade embellished paper
- ✿ ten 4mm silver-plated jump rings
- ✿ two sterling silver earring wires
- ✿ electric drill and small drill bit
- ✿ round-nose and long-nose pliers

**1** Select the area of the paper you want for your earrings and place the resin sticker on the paper. Cut around the sticker with a craft knife. Stick a second resin sticker to the back, sandwiching the paper to create a pebble.

**2** Use an electric drill with a small bit to make a hole in the top and bottom of each small resin pebble and in the top only of the large resin pebble. Repeat to make as many pebbles as you'll need for your earrings.

**3** Link the resin pebbles together with jump rings. Use the two pliers to open the jump rings sideways, rather than pulling them apart at the gap. Attach the top pebble to an earring wire. Repeat to make a second earring.

*techniques* basic tools... preparing for work

# button bangle

Bracelets are popular accessories, adding the perfect finishing touch to an outfit. If some of the bangles in your collection are looking outdated, here's a great way to give them a makeover with a ribbon-wrapping technique and some funky buttons.

## you will need ...

- ✿ assorted buttons in various sizes and colours
- ✿ plastic bangle bracelet
- ✿ felt for lining bracelet
- ✿ ribbon 6mm (¼in) wide x 2–3m (2–3yd)
- ✿ perle cotton 1m (1yd) in coordinating or contrasting colour
- ✿ strong craft glue

**1** Apply a dab of glue to the inside of the bracelet. Press the end of the ribbon firmly over the glue and allow it to dry. Start to wrap the ribbon around the bracelet, pulling tightly and overlapping each layer slightly. Cover the bracelet completely, ending on the inside and anchoring the ribbon end with glue.

**2** Thread the perle cotton on a needle, making a knot in the thread end. Take a small stitch in the ribbon on the inside of the bracelet. Bring the thread to the front and thread on two large buttons. Wrap the thread to the back at a slight angle and bring it to the front again. Thread three smaller buttons on and place this row close to the first row. Repeat wrapping and threading on buttons of various sizes. Take an occasional stitch through the ribbon on the inside to anchor the buttons. End with an anchor stitch and knot on the inside.

**3** Cut a strip of felt a little narrower than the inside of the bracelet and glue it in place, trimming the ends so they meet.

*techniques* basic tools... preparing for work... attaching buttons

# jeans bag

Now you don't have to throw away your favourite pair of jeans when they finally fall to bits – you can recycle them by making this cool backpack, giving them a second chance to look stylish! There are many details on jeans that can easily be incorporated into the bag, such as frayed hems, pockets and seams. Accessorize with your most fitted pair of jeans and you are ready to hit the town.

Useful and on trend – what more could you want from a bag? The appliqué here is really easy, using fusible web and scraps of pretty floral fabric. Complete the look with a matching bag charm and key ring.

## you will need ...

- 🌸 two pairs of denim jeans in different shades
- 🌸 pale blue gingham fabric 75 x 60cm (29½ x 24in)
- 🌸 large floral print cotton fabric
- 🌸 cream cord 150cm (60in)
- 🌸 blue grosgrain ribbon, 3cm (1¼in) wide

**1** To make a bag front and back, cut two pieces of denim from a pair of jeans, each 40 x 46cm (16 x 17½in). From the other jeans cut two pieces, each 40 x 14cm (16 x 5½in), using the bottom hem as a long edge. Using a strong needle in your machine, stitch the large pieces to the smaller ones along the long edge. Unpick a pocket from one of the pairs of jeans to go on the bag front.

**2** Iron fusible web on the back of the floral fabric and cut out two large flowers. Position on to the front panel and fuse the flowers in place. Sew the pocket in place, leaving the top open.

**3** Cut the waistbands from the jeans to form bag straps – two about 70cm (27½in) in length. Place the front and back panels right sides together and pin down the sides and along the bottom. Push the straps down into the bag and pin at the bottom corners. Sew along the sides and bottom, turn through to the right side and press flat.

**4** Make the lining by folding the gingham fabric in half along the long edge. Pin and sew along the side and bottom. Push the lining inside the bag. Fold the gingham over twice at the top so it covers the raw edge and pin in place. Pin the straps at the top beneath the gingham border and then sew along the top edge of the bag.

**5** Pin the blue ribbon around the bag top 6cm (2½in) down from the top edge, starting at the middle of the front and folding under the ribbon raw edges. Leave a 4cm (1½in) gap between the ends of the ribbon to form a drawstring channel. Sew the ribbon in place at the top and bottom edge. Use a safety pin to thread the cream cord through the drawstring channel to finish.

It's easy to make a bag charm and key ring. For a charm, sandwich a folded length of ribbon between two circles of denim, joined with fusible web. Iron on two fabric flowers and sew running stitch around the edge. For a key ring sew together a large flower and piece of denim the same size. Leave a gap and stuff with wadding. Put a folded length of thin ribbon into the gap and sew up. Edge with red stitches. Thread wooden beads on the ribbon and attach a key ring finding.

# magic mitten gloves

These two-way mitten gloves combine the versatility of fingerless gloves with the warmth of mittens. The gloves have been worked in different colours and the rich, autumnal shades used would look great throughout the season. Of course, you could knit them in a plain or variegated colour. Gloves are most successful when knitted in lightweight (DK) yarns. The yarn used here is 100% wool and knits up in stockinette stitch beautifully.

Working each mitten finger in a different colour adds a pleasingly quirky detail to these versatile gloves, and is also a great way to use up oddments of wool.

3

## you will need ...

✿ one 50g (1¾oz) lightweight (DK) wool yarn (120m/131yd per ball) in pumpkin (A), green (B), gold (C), yellow (D) and russet red (E)

✿ one pair size 3 (3.25mm) and one pair size 6 (4mm) knitting needles

✿ two small buttons

✿ stitch markers

## knitting notes...

The gauge is 22 sts and 28 rows to 10.2cm (4in) measured over stocking stitch using size 6 (4mm) needles. To fit sizes S [M:L]; width around palm is 18 [20.5:22]cm (7 [8:8½]in) and 18 [19:20.5]cm (7 [7½:8]in) long from wrist to top of mitten flap.

## knit the right glove

1 Using size 3 (3.25mm) needles and A, cast on 40 [44:48] sts.

• Row 1 *K1, p1; rep from * to end.

• Rep until rib is 6cm (2½in).

• Change to needle size 6 (4mm) and colour B and work 2 rows in st st (1 row k, 1 row p), starting with a k row.**

## 2 Shape the thumb gusset:

• Next Row K20 [22:24], M1, k2, M1, k18 [20:22]. 42 [46:50] sts.

• Work 3 rows in st st.

• Next Row K20 [22:24], M1, k4, M1, k18 [20:22]. 44 [48:52] sts.

• Work 3 rows in st st.

• Next Row K20 [22:24], M1, k6, M1, k18 [20:22]. 46 [50:54] sts.

• Work 3 rows in st st.

• Next Row K20 [22:24], M1, k8, M1, k18 [20:22]. 48 [52:56] sts.

• Work 3 rows in st st.

• Next Row K20 [22:24], M1, k10, M1, k18 [20:22]. 50 [54:58] sts.

• Purl 1 row.

## 3 Thumb:

• Next Row K32 [34:36], turn.

• Next Row, using C, cast on 2 sts, p14 (including last 2 sts just cast on), turn and cast on 2 sts.

• Using colour C, work 2.5cm (1in) on these 16 sts only for thumb, ending with a p row.

• Bind off. Join thumb seam.

• With RS of work facing, using size 6 (4mm) needles and B, pick up and k 2 sts across base of thumb, k across 18 [20:22] unworked sts on left-hand needle. 40 [44:48] sts.

• Work 2 rows. Place stitch markers on 2nd and 19th [21st:23rd] sts of last row.

***Cont in st st without shaping until work measures 4 [4.5:5]cm (1½ [1¾: 2]in) from pick-up sts at base of thumb, ending with a p row. Try the glove on; it should reach the base of your fingers. Add or subtract rows if needed to fit your hand length.

## 4 First finger:

• Next Row K25 [27:30] sts, turn.
• Next Row, using D, cast on 2 sts, p12 [12:14] (including 2 just cast on), turn and cast on 2 sts
• Using D, work 2.5cm (1in) on these 14 [14:16] sts only for first finger, ending with a p row.
• Bind off. Join finger seam.

## 5 Second finger:

• With RS of work facing, using size 6 (4mm) needles and C, pick up and k2 sts across base of first finger, k5 [6:6] and turn.

• Next Row, cast on 1 st, p13 [15:15] (including st just cast on), turn and cast on 1 st.
• Using C, work 2.5cm (1in) on these 14 [16:16] sts only for second finger, ending with p row.
• Bind off. Join finger seam.

## 6 Third finger:

• With RS of work facing, using size 6 (4mm) needles and A, pick up and k2 sts across base of second finger, k5 [6:6]. Turn.
• Next Row, cast on 1 st, p13 [15:15] (including st just cast

on), turn and cast on 1 st.
• Using A, work 2.5cm (1in) on these 14 [16:16] sts only for third finger, ending with a p row.
• Bind off. Join finger seam.

## 7 Fourth finger:

• With RS of work facing, using size 6 (4mm) needles and E, pick up and k4 sts across base of third finger, k across 5 [5:6] unworked sts to end.
• Next Row P across all 14 [14:16] rem sts.
• Using E, work 2.5cm (1in) on these 14 [14:16] sts only for fourth finger, ending with p row.
• Bind off. Join finger seam.

## 8 Mitten flap:

• Using size 3 (3.25mm) needles and E, cast on 20 [22:24] sts.
• Row 1 *K1, p1; rep from * to end.
• Rep this row 3 times more. Leave sts on a spare needle.

• With RS of work facing, using size 6 (4mm) needles and D, cast on 1 st then pick up and k18 [20:22] sts between markers on back of glove. 19 [21:23] sts.

• P 1 row.

• Next Row K19 [21:23] then k across 20 [22:24] sts of rib from spare needle. 39 [43:47] sts.

****Work in st st until flap measures 6 [9:9]cm (2½ [3½: 3½]in) from pick-up row, ending with a p row. Try on; the flap should be 2.5cm (1in) below the top of your longest finger. Add or subtract rows to fit your hand length if necessary.

**9 Shape the top:**

• Next Row K1, ssk, k14 [16:18], k3tog, ssk, k14 [16:18], k2tog, k1. 34 [38:42] sts.

• P 1 row.

• Next Row K1, (ssk, k12 [14:16], k2tog) twice, k1. 30 [34:38] sts.

For an easier project, instead of working the mitten gloves in bands of colours you could knit them in a pretty variegated shade of wool throughout.

• P 1 row.

• Next Row K1, (ssk, k10 [12:14], k2tog) twice, k1. 26 [30:34] sts.

• P 1 row.

• Next Row K1, (k3tog tbl, k6 [8:10], k3tog) twice, k1. 18 [22:26] sts.

• Bind off.

## knit the left glove

**10** Work as given for right glove (step 1) to **.

**11 Shape thumb gusset:**

• Next Row K18 [20:22], M1, k2,

M1, k20 [22:24]. 42 [46:50] sts.

• Work 3 rows in st st.

• Next Row K18 [20:22], M1, k4, M1, k20 [22:24]. 44 [48:52] sts.

• Work 3 rows in st st.

• Next Row K18 [20:22], M1, k6, M1, k20 [22:24]. 46 [50:54] sts.

• Work 3 rows in st st.

• Next Row K18 [20:22], M1, k8, M1, k20 [22:24]. 48 [52:56] sts.

• Work 3 rows in st st.

• Next Row K18 [20:22], M1, k10, M1, k20 [22:24]. 50 [54:58] sts.

• Purl 1 row.

**12 Thumb:**

• Next Row K30 [32:34] and turn.

• Next Row, using C, cast on 2 sts (using cable cast-on), p14 (including last 2 sts just cast on), turn and cast on 2 sts.

• Using C, work 2.5cm (1in) on these 16 sts only for thumb, ending with a p row.

• Bind off. Join thumb seam.

• With RS of work facing using size 6 (4mm) needles and B, pick up and k2 sts across base of thumb, k20 [22:24] unworked sts on left-hand needle. 40 [44:48] sts.

• Work 2 rows. Place markers on the 22nd [24th:26th] and 39th [43rd:47th] sts of the last row.

• Work as given for the right glove from ***.

**13 Mitten flap:**

• Using size 3 (3.25mm) needles and E, cast on 20 [22:24] sts loosely.

• Row 1 *K1, p1; rep from * to end.

• Rep this row 3 times more. Leave these sts on a spare needle.

• With RS of work facing, using size 6 (4mm) needles and D, pick up and k18 [20:22] sts between markers on back of glove.

• Next Row, cast on 1 st, p to end. 19 [21:22] sts.

• K 1 row.

• Next Row P19 [21:23] then p across 20 [22:24] sts of rib from spare needle. 39 [43:47] sts.

• Complete as given for mitten flap of right glove from ****.

## finish off

**14** To finish, sew in all yarn ends. Join the top seam of the mitten flap. Join the side seam of the flap to the top of rib. Sew each end of the rib flat on to the glove. Join the side seam of the glove. Make a small loop in the middle of the top of the flap, using 2 strands of D. Work buttonhole stitch evenly over the loop. Fold the flap over on to the back of glove, mark the position of the loop and sew on a small button.

*techniques* basic tools... preparing for work... knitting techniques... knitting mittens and gloves... buttonhole stitch

# simple socks

These funky tube socks are perfect for first-time sock knitters because there's no heel to turn and no shaping until the simple decreases for the toe. The support around the heel comes from the ribbed pattern that creates elasticity, hugging the contours of your foot. The socks are knitted in the round with double-pointed needles to form a tube so you can make them any length you like – just stop when you've had enough!

To liven up your learning process, work your socks in some funky, eye-popping colours, as brash and bright as you like. The red, pink and yellow bands on these purple socks create great contrast.

## you will need ...

✿ lightweight (DK) wool, acrylic
  and nylon mix yarn:

  one 50g (1¾oz) ball in purple (A)

  one 50g (1¾oz) ball in red (B)

  one 50g (1¾oz) ball in pink (C)

  one 50g (1¾oz) ball in yellow (D)

✿ double-pointed knitting needles:
  one set size 1 (2.5mm) and one
  set size 4 (3.5mm)

✿ stitch marker

## knitting notes...

Achieving an exact gauge is not
essential here because the ribbing
makes the knitted fabric stretchy.
To fit three calf widths of small
[medium: large]. The overall length
of a sock is 53cm (20½in) but can
be worked longer or shorter.

## knit your socks

**1** (Make 2). Cast on 45 [51: 57] sts in yarn A using
size 1 (2.5mm) double-pointed needles. Evenly
distribute sts over 3 needles and place a stitch marker
to indicate the beginning of the round. Now work in
the round, taking care not to twist sts.

• Round 1 (K2, p1) to end of round.

• Cont as set until knitting measures 2.5cm (1in).

• Change to size 4 (3.5mm) double-pointed needles.

## work the coloured bands

**2** Four wide bands of colour are worked around the
calf and four narrower bands at the toe. (Make 2)

• Work 8 rounds in yarn B, 8 rounds in yarn C and 8
rounds in yarn D.

• Change to yarn A and cont until work measures
44cm (17½in).

• Work 4 rows in yarn B, 4 rows in yarn C and 4 rows
in yarn D.

• Now change to yarn A and size 1 (2.5mm) double-
pointed needles.

There's no shaping at all in these tube
socks until you decrease for the toe
– instead, the stretchy ribbing will mould
the sock to your foot contours.

## shape the toe

**3** Work 3 rounds in pattern.

• Next round (K2tog, p1) to end of round.

• Work 3 more rounds.

• Next round K2tog to end of round.

• K 1 round.

**4** Transfer sts to two double-pointed needles and graft rem sts, as follows. Cut the yarn leaving about 30cm (12in) to graft with. Thread the yarn on to a darning needle. Insert the darning needle purlwise into the first stitch on the front needle and pull the yarn through. Insert the needle knitwise into the first stitch on the back needle and pull the yarn through.

* Insert the needle knitwise into the first stitch on the front needle and slip the stitch off the needle. Insert the needle purlwise into the next stitch on the front needle and pull the yarn through. Insert the needle purlwise into the first stitch on the back needle and slip this stitch off the needle. Insert the needle knitwise into the next stitch on the back

needle and pull the yarn through*. Repeat from * to * until all the stitches are grafted. Darn in any loose ends to finish.

# ballerina slippers

Get in touch with your inner diva and take a twirl in these gorgeous slippers. Modelled on the classic, elegant shape of ballet shoes, they're perfect for keeping your feet comfy and stylish at home. They're easy to create as they are knitted flat on straight needles, with the two sides of the heel seamed together to create the shape. Make a whole collection in your favourite colours!

There are many ways to make your ballet slippers beautiful, such as the artificial flowers used here. Experiment with other jazzy embellishments, such as shiny sequins and beads, quirky buttons and flamboyant embroidery using bright threads.

## you will need ...

- ❀ one 100g (3½oz) ball of lightweight (DK) acrylic yarn in bright pink
- ❀ one pair of size 6 (4mm) knitting needles
- ❀ one size G6 (4mm) crochet hook
- ❀ two artificial flowers
- ❀ two contrasting beads for flower centres

## knitting notes...

The gauge is 22 sts and 30 rows to 10.2cm (4in) square measured over st st using size 6 (4mm) needles.
To fit three sizes: small [medium: large].

# knit your slippers

**1 Sole:** (Make 2). Cast on 12 [12: 14] sts using size 6 (4mm) needles.

- Row 1 K.
- Row 2 P1, pfb, k8 [8: 10], pfb, p1. 14 [14: 16] sts.
- Row 3 K.
- Row 4 P1, pfb, k10 [10: 12], pfb, p1. 16 [16: 18] sts.
- Row 5 K.
- Row 6 P1, pfb, k12 [12: 14], pfb, p1. 18 [18: 20] sts.**
- Work 53 [55: 57] rows in st st.
- Next row P1, p2tog, k10 [12: 14], p2tog tbl, p1. 16 [16: 18] sts.
- Next row K.
- Next row P1, p2tog, k8 [10: 12], p2tog tbl, p1. 14 [14: 16] sts.

*The slippers are knitted flat on straight needles and then the two sides of the heel are seamed together.*

- Next row K.
- Next row P1, p2tog, k6 [8: 10], p2tog tbl, p1. 12 [12: 14] sts.
- Next row K.
- Bind off.

**2 Top of slipper:**

- Work as for sole to **.
- Work 18 rows in st st.
- Next row K8 [8: 9] sts, bind off 2 sts, k8 [8: 9] sts. 16 [16: 18] sts.
- Next row, working on first 8 [8: 9] sts only, p.
- Next row K2tog tbl, k to end. 7 [7: 8] sts.
- Next row P.
- Next row K2tog tbl, k to end. 6 [6: 7] sts.
- Next row P.
- Work 10 [10: 12] rows in st st ending on P row.

*Acrylic yarn was used so the slippers can be washed in the machine. However, you could make them in a more luxurious lightweight (DK) yarn.*

- Next row K1, m1, k5 [5: 6] sts. 7 [7: 8] sts.
- Work 7 rows in st st.
- Next row K1, m1, k6 [6: 7] sts. 8 [8: 9] sts.
- Work 9 rows in st st.
- Next row K1, m1, k7 [7: 8] sts. 9 [9: 10] sts.
- Next row P.
- Bind off.
- Re-join yarn to remaining sts and repeat for other side, reversing shapings.

## making up

**3** With right sides facing, join the sole to the top of the foot – see Sewing Up in Knitting Techniques.

## work the crochet edging

Note: The crochet instructions are given in US terms – see Crochet Techniques for UK terms.

**4** With crochet hook size G6 (4mm) work a round of single crochet in a number divisible by 4.

- Next round, chain 1, work 2 sc into next 2 sts, * miss 1 st, work 3 sc, rep from * to end. Fasten off.

**5** Sew an artificial flower to the slipper and secure with sewing thread and a contrasting bead.

## crochet as embellishment...

Crochet is a lovely way to add design flourishes to knitted items. The slipper trim is worked around the edge of the knitted cuff. Decide where you're going to start the crochet round. Insert the crochet hook beneath both the horizontal strands of yarn at the top of one knitted stitch. Make a slipknot in the working end of the yarn, and place the loop of the slipknot on the crochet hook. Pull this loop through the knitted fabric. Now start to crochet.

groovy gifts

# fabric frames

You can never have too many picture frames and with these little fabric-covered frames even the smallest snapshots can be beautifully displayed. Be bold with your choice of main patterned print and select simple coordinating fabrics. Pulp board picture frame blanks available from many craft stores make the perfect base – these were 10.2 x 15.2cm (4 x 6in). Add yo-yos to the corners of each frame to link the three frames together, or use bright, artificial flowers instead.

A trio of frames in coordinating fabrics makes an attractive display for some favourite photos and these frames are embellished further with gathered fabric yo-yos, each finished off with sequins and beads in the centre.

## you will need ...

- ✿ fabrics in bold print, pink spot print and blue spot print
- ✿ three pulp board picture frame blanks
- ✿ ribbons in pink and blue (long enough for the inside of the frame)
- ✿ seed beads and sequins
- ✿ vanishing marker
- ✿ printed papers for backing
- ✿ double-sided tape and glue stick
- ✿ yo-yo maker (optional)

Be creative with your choice of fabrics and decoration for a unique look! Try cotton or denim fabrics from old clothing. Experiment with colours and go bold with fluorescent shades. Decorate the frames as much as you like, perhaps with fabric paints or unusual embellishments, such as feathers.

**1** Use a craft knife to cut around the sides and bottom of the frame to separate the back panel if necessary. Cut a piece of fabric larger than the frame and draw around the frame on to this fabric using a vanishing marker.

**2** When using the bold print fabric, decorate by adding seed beads and sequins, stitching them around the area that will cover the frame.

**3** Draw a cross in the centre of the fabric, to mark out the frame window. Cut diagonally from corner to corner to leave four triangular flaps. Use double-sided tape to stick the fabric to the frame. Fold the overhanging fabric over the edges to the back of the frame and secure with tape.

**4** Cover the inside edges of the frame with ribbon to hide raw edges at the inside corners. Stick in place with double-sided tape. Cut out a piece of coordinating printed paper and stick on to the back panel using a glue stick. Make the other frames in the same way.

**5** Use bold printed fabric to make three yo-yos for each spotted frame, following the manufacturer's instructions. Press the yo-yo flat with a warm iron. In the centre of each yo-yo, sew a large sequin, a smaller one and a seed bead.

If you don't have a yo-yo maker create your own yo-yos as follows. Cut a circle of fabric 20.3cm (8in) in diameter. Fold the edge over by 6mm (¼in) and sew a running stitch around the circle. Pull the thread to gather up the edge and secure with a small stitch. Press flat with an iron.

**6** Stick the front of the frame to the back along the side and bottom edges using either strong glue or double-sided tape. Arrange three yo-yos in the bottom corner of the frame and secure in place with double-sided tape.

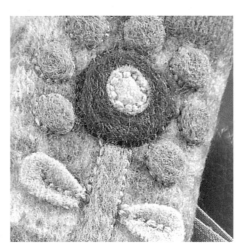

# ipod sweater

This project is great fun and perfect if you have a jumper that has already been accidentally felted when it was washed! The little iPod sweater is soft and snug, small enough to tuck into your jean's pocket or bag – it should protect and extend the life of your iPod too. For an inexpensive make, look for 100% wool sweaters in secondhand shops (thrift stores) in a colour and pattern you like.

Wool roving was used to add decoration to the project in a sweet flower design using a needle-felting technique. Why not make up a simple design of your own?

## you will need ...

❀ 100% wool sweater

❀ wool rovings in green, pink and blue

❀ green wool felt

❀ embroidery cotton (floss) in pale green

❀ needle-felting needle

❀ needle-felting foam

**1** Machine wash the sweater and dry in the dryer to felt the fibres and shrink the sweater. Copy the template provided and lay the rectangle on the sweater with the top of the pattern lined up with the hem. Cut out two sweater pieces.

Rovings are combed pieces of wool drawn into a clump and twisted to hold the fibres together prior to spinning. You will find lots of lovely colours at your local craft shop – try variegated colours too!

**2** Lay the front piece down on a piece of needle-felting foam. Pull out a piece of green roving and lay it on the sweater for the flower stem, following the pattern. Begin felting by inserting a felting needle into the roving and, holding it straight, jab it in and out through the sweater, down to the foam. This will bond the fibres to each other and the sweater. Check the fibres are coming through to the back. Continue felting along the sides and through the middle until the wool is in a firm design against the sweater. Pull out a small bit of pink wool roving for the flower centre, roll it into a smooth ball, lay it in place and needle felt it. Use blue roving to felt the petals using the pattern as a guide.

**3** Cut two green leaves from green wool felt and using six strands of embroidery cotton and back-stitch, stitch them to the stem. Using six strands of thread, backstitch around the stem, flower centre and petals to outline them.

**4** Lay the two sweater pieces right sides together and sew around three sides, leaving the top open. Sew around again, just outside the first stitching line. Trim away excess seam allowance close to the second line of stitching and turn right side out. Slip your iPod inside to test for a snug fit, adjusting the seam allowance if necessary.

You could add your own touches to the design, perhaps changing the petal shapes or adding a white circle of wool felt in the centre of the flower.

*techniques* basic tools... preparing for work... templates

# dishy delight

This little trinket dish would look cute on a bedside table and is a lovely way to use up favourite fabrics. The flowers are easily created, while pearly buttons add an attractive finishing touch. The finished size is approximately 10.2cm (4in) square.

**you will need ...**

✿ two 20.3cm (8in) squares of fabric and scraps of two other patterns

✿ iron-on stabilizer for backing

✿ fusible web

✿ five buttons

**1** Use the template provided to trace the dish outline on to iron-on stabilizer, following the solid outer line. Cut out and iron on to the back of a patterned fabric. Cut out the patterned fabric so it is 1cm (⅜in) larger all the way around. Fold in the fabric edges and press flat.

**2** Trace the smaller dish outline shape on to fusible web, following the dashed lines. Iron on to a different fabric and cut out. Peel off the backing, place on the larger shape so it covers the folded edges and iron in place. Fold up the sides of the dish and sew together at the side seams with tiny stitches.

**3** With the two patterned scraps, use fusible web to stick the same fabrics together, so the same print is on either side. Use the templates to cut four small flowers from one piece and one large flower from the other. Sew the small flowers to the corners of the dish, securing in place with a button. Sew the larger flower in the centre of the dish with a button in the middle.

*techniques* basic tools... preparing for work... using fusible web... templates

# pucker-up purse

If every type of yarn represented a place, then Lurex would have to be Las Vegas – twinkly, bright and a little bit trashy! It's used here to create this glamorous accessory. The inspiration for the purse came from Salvador Dali's legendary Mae West Lips sofa, and the purse is knitted in an appropriately bright red colour. It would also make a great gift if knitted in a blush pink or rich burgundy colour and filled with glamorous make-up.

This sexy purse is knitted in easy stockinette (stocking) stitch. The pouting effect is created with short rows, which gives the knitted fabric a three-dimensional shape and a lovely curvy outline.

## you will need ...

- ✿ two 50g (1¾oz) balls of fine-weight (4ply) Lurex yarn
- ✿ one pair of size 3 (3.25mm) knitting needles
- ✿ stitch holder
- ✿ 51cm (20in) square of toning fabric for lining
- ✿ zip 18cm (7in) long
- ✿ toy stuffing (optional)

## knitting notes...

The gauge is 26 sts and 40 rows to 10.2cm (4in) square over stockinette stitch using size 3 (3.25mm) needles. The yarn is used double (knit through both strands of yarn for each stitch). The front and back are different sizes.

## knitting the purse

**1 Front:** Cast on 20 sts.

- Row 1 Inc 1, k20, inc 1. 22 sts.
- Row 2 and every even row until zip shaping, purl.
- Row 3 Inc 1, k5, m1, k12, m1, k5, inc 1. 26 sts.
- Row 5 Inc 1, k26, inc 1. 28 sts.
- Row 7 Inc 1, k22, turn, ss, p15, turn, ss, knit to end, inc 1. 30 sts.
- Row 9 Inc 1, k30, inc 1. 32 sts.
- Row 11 Inc 1, k6, m1, k20, m1, k6, inc 1. 36 sts.
- Row 13 Inc 1, k36, inc 1. 38 sts.
- Row 15 Inc 1, k28, turn, ss, p17, turn, ss, knit to end, inc 1. 40 sts.
- Row 17 Inc 1, k40, inc 1. 42 sts.
- Row 19 Inc 1, k7, m1, k28, m1, k7, inc 1. 46 sts.
- Row 21 Inc 1, k46, inc 1. 48 sts.
- Row 23 Inc 1, k34, turn, ss, p19, turn, ss, knit to end, inc 1. 50 sts.
- Row 25 Inc 1, k50, inc 1. 52 sts.
- Row 27 Inc 1, k15, k2tog tbl, k18, k2tog, k15, inc 1. 52 sts.
- Repeat last 2 rows twice more, then purl 1 row.

## 2 Zip shaping:

- Row 33 K4 and working only on these sts, work 3 rows. Cut yarn and place these sts on stitch holder.
- With RS facing, re-join yarn to stitches and work on centre 44 sts. Purl 1 row to create a ridge.
- Work 3 rows in st st. Bind off.
- Cast on 44 sts and work 3 rows in st st, starting with a knit row.
- Work 1 knit row to create a ridge, then place the sts on a stitch holder and cut yarn.
- Re-join yarn to remaining 4 sts and work 3 rows.
- Next row, knit across these 4 sts, the 44 cast-on stitches, and across the 4 sts held on stitch holder.
- Work 2 rows in st st, no shaping.

## 3 Upper lip:

- Row 1 K2tog, k15, m1, k18, m1, k15, k2tog. 52 sts.
- Row 2 and every even row until row 24, purl.
- Rows 3 and 5, as row 1.
- Row 7 K2tog, k33, turn, ss, p18,

turn, ss, knit to last 2 sts, k2tog. 50 sts.
• Row 9 K2tog, k33, turn, ss, p16, turn, ss, knit to last 2 sts, k2tog. 48 sts.
• Row 11 K2tog, k22, turn and work on these stitches, leaving remaining stitches on stitch holder.
• Row 13 K2tog, k18, k2tog. 20 sts.
• Row 15 K2tog, k15, turn, ss, p13, turn, ss, knit to last 2 sts, k2tog. 18 sts.
• Row 17 K2tog, k14, k2tog. 16 sts.
• Row 19 K2tog, k10, turn, ss, p7, turn, ss, knit to last 2 sts, k2tog. 14 sts.
• Row 21 K2tog, k12, k2tog. 12 sts.
• Row 23 K2tog, k10, k2tog. 10 sts.
• Row 24, bind off 2 sts, p6, p2tog. 9 sts. Bind off remaining stitches.
• RS facing, re-join yarn to stitches on stitch holder (row 11), and work to match, reversing all shaping.

**4 Back:** Cast on 20 sts.
• Work in st st, starting with knit row.
• Increase on next (Row 3) and every

following knit row until 54 sts.
• Work 5 rows st st, no shaping.
• Decrease (use k2tog) at each end of every knit row until 46 sts.
• Purl 1 row.
• Row 1 K2tog, k21, turn and work on these stitches, leaving remaining stitches on a stitch holder.
• Row 2 and every even row until row 16, purl.
• Row 3 K2tog, k18, k2tog. 20 sts.
• Row 5 K2tog, knit to end. 19 sts.
• Row 7 K2tog, k15, k2tog. 17 sts.
• Row 9 K2tog, k13, k2tog. 15 sts.
• Row 11 K2tog, k11, k2tog. 13 sts.
• Row 13 K2tog, k9, k2tog. 11 sts.
• Row 15, bind off 2 sts, k6, k2tog. 8 sts.
• Row 16 P2tog, p6. 7 sts.
• Bind off the remaining stitches. With RS facing, re-join yarn to the stitches on stitch holder and work to match, reversing all shaping.

## making up

**5** Darn in loose ends and press gently. Using the knitted pieces as templates, cut out two lining pieces, marking the front opening. Pin the zip on the wrong side of the lining to correspond with the opening. Slit the fabric to correspond with the zip's teeth. Re-pin the lining, hemming it and slipstitching it on to the zip. Place the lining pieces right sides together and stitch together.

**6** Pin the knitted pieces wrong sides together, adjusting pins around edges for best fit. Stitch around the edges of the lip shape. Insert the lining lips into the knitted lips. Pad the lips with stuffing. Slipstitch the zip to the edges of the knitted front.

# birdie album

This photo album cover was inspired by colourful vintage crewel embroidery. By using bright colours and outlining the design in wool (yarn), you can achieve this look without working even one stitch. Wool felt is used as the base fabric since it won't fray and is very forgiving to work with (no sewing required!). This idea would be great for any photo album, journal or scrapbook.

This bird design is very simple but looks fabulous in these bold colours. You could also design your own cover. Flip through embroidery books or clip-art images to find fun designs and then replicate the design in felt.

## you will need ...

- ✿ wool roving in dark turquoise, olive green and orange
- ✿ wool felt in light blue, large enough to cover the album
- ✿ wool yarn in brown and hot pink
- ✿ photo album at least 14 x 18cm (5½ x 7in)
- ✿ pinking shears
- ✿ felting needle
- ✿ foam work surface
- ✿ air-soluble marking pen
- ✿ fabric transfer paper
- ✿ fabric gluer

**1** Open the album and lay it on the light blue felt. Measure around the album: flush with the top and bottom edges but add 7.6cm (3in) on each side to create flaps to attach to the inside of the front and back covers. Mark the measured rectangle with an air-soluble pen and cut out with pinking shears. Wrap the rectangle around the closed album and fold the end flaps inside the front and back covers. To determine the boundaries of the design, use an air-soluble pen to mark the left and right edges of the front cover.

**2** Photocopy the template provided. Depending on the size of your album, you may need to enlarge the template. Use fabric transfer paper to transfer the design between the marked lines on the cut blue felt.

Instead of an album cover you could work the design on a larger piece of felt and make it up into a little bag – ideal to store jewellery or other trinkets.

**3** Lay the rectangle on a foam work surface (not on the album). Take the dark turquoise wool roving, pull off tufts and lay on the rectangle in even layers, covering the area to be felted, starting with the bird's body. Insert a felting needle into the roving and, holding it straight, jab it in and out through the foundation, down to the foam. This will bond the fibres to each other and to the foundation – check that the fibres are coming through to the back. Fill in the body design, needle felting until it's smooth. Repeat for the olive green and orange colours in the rest of the design.

**4** Lay the hot pink wool yarn around the bird, circles and leaves. Needle felt the yarn to attach it to the felt cover. Now needle felt the brown yarn to the cover to create a branch.

**5** Use fabric glue to stick the needle-felted cover to the photo album. Finish by folding and securing the flaps inside the front and back covers of the album.

# retro cards

Painting bright swirling shapes on to white card creates fabulous motifs and would make great cards for Valentine's Day. Instead of painting a swirly design yourself with acrylic paints you could simply use patterned paper or a rubber stamp.

## you will need ...

- ❀ sheets of and white card
- ❀ scrap of white card for heart
- ❀ tracing paper
- ❀ acrylic paints in fuchsia, apricot and yellow
- ❀ narrow magenta ribbon
- ❀ pink outliner

**1** Transfer the design from the template provided, using tracing paper and a soft pencil (or design your own pattern). Colour with acrylic paint in fuchsia, apricot and yellow shades. Leave to dry.

**2** Trim the pink card and fold it in half to make a tall card blank. Cut or punch a patterned heart, pierce a hole at the top and thread through a length of magenta ribbon. Glue to the centre of the card blank so the heart hangs free. Embellish the ribbon with dots of pink outliner.

**3** For an alternative look, cut and fold a tall, white card blank. Paint the swirly pattern, as before and then cut into three sections. Glue each piece on the card, one above the other, with equal spacing between the parts.

*techniques* basic tools... preparing for work... papercraft techniques... templates

# cake slice

This celebratory cake slice, complete with candle would be a fun gift for a friend's birthday. The basic cake slice is made from lightweight oiled stencil card, which is highly flexible, yet very strong. The top is covered with frosted paper, complete with a sprinkling of 'hundreds and thousands', while strips of red and white paper create the effect of a cream and jam filling. You could use little brown or red buttons instead, to imitate chocolate drops or cherries on the top.

The cake slice is given extra decoration by the addition of a candle, made by rolling paper, wrapped in a gold spiral and complete with flame.

## you will need ...

✿ A4 (US letter) sheet of lightweight oiled stencil card

✿ A4 (US letter) sheet of white medium-weight card

✿ A4 (US letter) sheet of frosted pink paper

✿ A4 (US letter) sheet of brown paper

✿ narrow strip of white paper

✿ narrow strip of red paper

✿ very thin strip of gold paper

✿ half a sheet of blue paper

✿ scraps of yellow and orange paper for flame

✿ scraps of red, pink and brown paper for hundreds and thousands

*Where card or paper pieces have to be joined, make sure to line up the joins at the back, to make them as inconspicuous as possible.*

**1** For the cake slice base, use the segment template, enlarged by 200%. Trace the shape on to the stencil card and cut out. For the sides, cut a strip of stencil card 11.2 x 34.3cm (4⅜ x 13½in) (joining as necessary). Crease a 1cm (⅜in) border along one long edge of the strip. With scissors, snip regularly into the 1cm (⅜in) border. Fold the snips over so the shape will curve and then glue it on the base segment shape, around the edge.

**2** Use the segment template again and white card to make a segment shape but make it 1cm (⅜in) bigger all round. Crease a 1cm (⅜in) border all round, cut snips into this and fold the edge over. Cover the top in frosted pink paper. Snip strips of plain red, pink and brown paper for 'hundreds and thousands' and glue them to the pink paper. Glue the whole shape inside the top of the cake slice. You now have a three-dimensional slice.

**3** Use the scalloped template and white card to create a strip about 34.3cm (13½in) long, joining as necessary. Glue this around the sides of the cake slice, so the scallops are just above the top edge.

**4** Cut a 9 x 34.3cm (3½ x 13½in) strip of brown paper and glue it to the sides of the cake all round. For the cream and jam 'filling', cut a 2.5 x 34.3cm (1 x 13½in) strip of white paper and glue it in the centre of the brown strip all round. Cut a 1.5 x 34.3cm (½ x 13½in) strip of red paper and glue it in the centre of the white strip all round.

**5** For the candle, cut an 8 x 10.2cm (3⅛ x 4in) strip of blue paper. Roll the paper around a pencil or pen to make a tube and stick the ends in place with double-sided tape. Slip the tube off the pencil. Glue a very thin strip of gold paper in a spiral around the candle.

**6** Using the flame template, cut the outer shape from yellow paper and inner shape from orange paper. Score and crease where marked. Glue the

flame together, then glue the flame inside the candle. Glue the candle to the top of the cake.

# tempting treats

# stuffed chicks

These cute chicks are really easy to create from fabric scraps and would make great mascots for a desk top. It is always a surprise to add the faces at the end and discover each bird's personality. You could make a whole collection to give to friends and embroider their names on the chicks' backs.

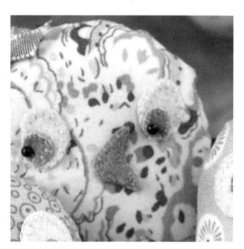

The chicks develop personalities as you add their features, so try out a few different looks. It's also easy to customize a chick with little embellishments — try tiny bows, bells or rosebuds.

## you will need ...

* cotton fabrics
* wool felt scraps in different colours
* round black beads
* embroidery cotton (floss)
* polyester toy stuffing
* little ribbons or bells (optional)

**1** To make one chick, trace the templates provided to make paper patterns and cut two bodies and four wings from cotton fabric. From small pieces of felt in different colours cut two eyes, a beak and two feet. There are three choices of beak shape and two wing shapes.

**2** Pin the wing pieces right sides together. Sew around the stitching lines using a short stitch length on your sewing machine. Turn the wings right side out and stuff with toy stuffing. Pin the wings in place, sandwiched between the two body pieces with right sides together.

**3** Sew around the body, leaving an opening at the bottom, as shown on the template. Clip around the curved edges so the seam won't pucker. Turn the body right side out and fill the chick with toy stuffing. Sew the opening closed with a needle and thread.

**4** Sew the eyes, beak and feet in place by hand using one strand of matching embroidery cotton and blanket stitch.

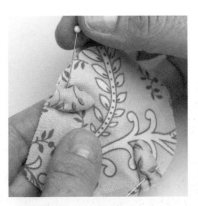

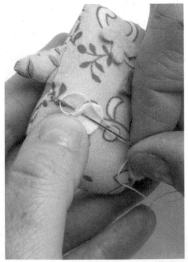

**5** Using a thin needle and strong thread, sew tiny black beads on the eyes. Finish by adding a tiny ribbon bow or bell if you like.

It's easy to design your own little chicks, such as this cute owlet. Start by drawing a simple outline, adding feet, limbs and features. Use cotton fabric for the body. Cut facial features from felt and embroider the details. Try it with other animals too.

# neapolitan soap pops

You'll be hooked on soap making once you've made these delicious looking soaps. The style is both nostalgic and classic, and surely everyone loves Neapolitan ice cream! This ice cream will be really popular with all your friends too – perfect to give as quick gifts, plus they're scented with gorgeous strawberry and chocolate. This project makes eight 85g (3oz) soap pops.

The pink, white and chocolate colouring of Neapolitan ice cream is perfect for these yummy soap pops – good enough to eat! You'll want to experiment with other colour combinations too.

## you will need ...

✿ 470ml (16fl oz) (2-cup) microwave-safe glass measuring cup

✿ 510g (18oz) white soap base

✿ 255g (9oz) clear soap base

✿ brown oxide soap pigment

✿ nonbleeding liquid red soap colourant

✿ 2.5ml (½ teaspoon) strawberry fragrance oil

✿ 2.5ml (½ teaspoon) chocolate fragrance oil

✿ eight plastic freezer pop moulds 85g (3oz) capacity

✿ rubbing alcohol in spray bottle

✿ eight wooden craft sticks

✿ soap thermometer

✿ small saucepan

**1** In the microwave-safe glass measuring cup, melt 255g (9oz) of white soap base. Add the red colourant one drop at a time, stirring with a craft stick each time until you get a pink colour. Add the strawberry fragrance oil and stir well. Fill eight pop moulds each one third full and allow to set to room temperature.

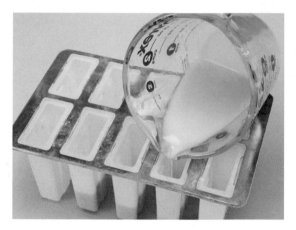

Liberally spray the hot soap with rubbing alcohol after pouring each layer into the moulds to remove all the bubbles. If any remain, they will be visible on the finished soaps.

**2** Melt 255g (9oz) of white soap base. Allow the soap to cool to 49°C (120°F). Spray the pink soap in the moulds with rubbing alcohol. Pour white soap in until each mould is two-thirds full. Spray with rubbing alcohol and allow the soaps to set to room temperature.

**3** Melt 255g (9oz) of clear soap base and add the brown pigment (as you did with the red colourant) for a chocolate colour. Add the chocolate fragrance oil. Spray the white soap in each mould with rubbing alcohol. Pour the brown soap into each mould, to within 3mm (⅛in) of the top edge. Spray the tops of the soaps with rubbing alcohol.

**4** Insert the sticks through the melted brown soap into the firmer white soap, leaving about 5cm (2in) sticking out. To make sure sticks are centred, put them in at eye level and check the positions from the side too. Put the moulds in the freezer for half an hour.

**5** Remove from the freezer and separate the individual soap moulds. To unmould the soaps, put about four cups of boiling water in a small saucepan. While holding on to the sticks, dunk each mould into the water for four seconds or so. Remove from the water and pull on the stick to remove the soap.

# birthday bunting

These cute felt motifs can either be hung as a bunting or used individually as gift tags on a birthday or Christmas present, adding a handmade touch. They are really quick to make using scraps of felt and assorted beads and sequins.

## you will need ...

- ✿ felt in yellow, pink and blue for the cupcake
- ✿ felt in brown and green for the gingerbread man
- ✿ assorted sequins, seed beads and bugle beads
- ✿ mini metallic pegs (optional)
- ✿ length of bright ribbon for hanging

**1** Use the templates provided to cut two of each shape from the coloured felts. Only cut one star.

**2** For the cupcake, glue or catch stitch the pink felt piece to the centre of the blue piece. Using matching sewing thread, sew random sequins over the cake base and a line of bugle beads on each side of the pink felt. Sew short bugle beads or seed beads randomly over the yellow felt. Sew the yellow top to the cupcake base.

**3** For the gingerbread man, sew the star to his chest with running stitches and add random sequins all over. Add two sequins for eyes, each with a seed bead in the centre.

**4** For both motifs, match up a plain felt shape with a decorated shape and sew together all around the edge using buttonhole stitch. Make as many motifs as you like and hang them on the ribbon with mini pegs.

*techniques* basic tools... preparing for work... attaching beads... templates

# button baby dolls

These button dolls are such fun to create and make great handbag charms. You could use strands of embroidery cotton on the head for hair.

**you will need ...**

- ✿ fifty or more flat buttons in a variety of sizes and colours
- ✿ embroidery cotton (floss) 132cm (52in)
- ✿ seam sealant

**1** Cut two lengths of cotton 51cm (20in) long, lay together and fold in half. Tie all the strands together at the folded end. Choose four large buttons for a hat. Thread pairs of threads through separate (and opposite) holes in the buttons. Choose three slightly smaller buttons for the face and add below the hat brim.

**2** Use ten to fifteen buttons for the body. To stack a dress, start with smaller buttons and graduate to larger ones. Or arrange the buttons to be trousers (pants) and a shirt – see picture for ideas. Thread the stacks on the cotton, stopping when you get to the legs. To add legs or trousers, separate each of the double strands into individual strands and thread these through each of the two stacks of about ten buttons. Add socks and shoes if you choose. At the bottom of each leg, tie the two strands in a square knot. Seal the knots with seam sealant.

**3** For the arms, cut two 15.2cm (6in) lengths of cotton. Lay side by side, insert them between the second and third body buttons, and tie a square knot around the cotton in the centre of the body. Using two strands, thread about ten buttons on each side to form the arms and hands. Knot and seal as before.

---

*techniques* basic tools... preparing for work

# funky flowers

A whole mix of fun, vibrant colours and bold forms was used to create this funky bouquet of flowers – perfect to give as an unusual gift or to decorate your home. Bright die-cut blooms combined with smaller flowers are enhanced by a dotty relief pattern and contrasting punched centres. The flowers are attached to fluorescent-coloured looped drinking straws tied with ribbon and displayed in a glass vase with a flamboyant ribbon bow.

You can give your flowers extra pizzazz by adding little ribbon bows to the centres and adding dots of dimensional fluid to create an interesting surface patterning. Curling the petals adds a further dimension.

## you will need ...

- ✿ die-cut card daisies in large and medium
- ✿ card in contrasting colours to the daisies
- ✿ narrow ribbon in colours to match/coordinate with daisies
- ✿ wide ribbon in spotted green sheer
- ✿ coloured looped drinking straws
- ✿ dimensional fluid
- ✿ circle punches in medium and small
- ✿ die-cutting system and circles embossing folder
- ✿ glass vase and coloured marbles

*Instead of using an embossing folder you could buy coloured card that is already embossed and cut your own daisy shapes.*

**1** Apply dots of dimensional fluid all over the petals of the large die-cut daisies but not to the flower centres. Leave to dry for about twenty minutes.

**2** Using the medium circle punch, punch circles from contrasting-coloured card for the centres of the large daisies. Punch two small holes in the centre of each circle. Thread each flower centre with a length of ribbon in a colour to coordinate with the petals, tie in a knot and trim the ends at an angle.

**3** Place each medium daisy in turn into the embossing folder, insert into the die-cutting system and press down to emboss the circles pattern (see photo opposite, top left).

**4** Curl the end of each petal by stretching it around a pen. Using the small circle punch, punch circles from contrasting-coloured card for medium daisy centres and glue in place. Apply a coat of dimensional fluid over each centre and leave to dry.

**5** Attach a drinking straw in a contrasting colour to the back of one petal of each large daisy using double-sided tape. Using the medium circle punch, punch a circle from card to match the colour of the petals of each flower and glue to the back of the petals, to cover the end of the straw as pictured above right.

**6** Tie a length of the patterned or sheer ribbon to each of the straw stems on one side of the loops. Glue an embossed daisy on the opposite side of the loop and leave to dry. Wrap the spotted green sheer ribbon around the vase and tie in a bow. Put glass marbles in the base of the vase and arrange the flowers to hold the stems in position.

# cupcake bag

This handbag looks good enough to eat! Grey felt was used to make the bag, which doesn't fray so there's no need for hems. The dark felt also makes a nice contrast to the pretty, candy-coloured fabrics used for the appliqué. The candy striped handles add to the fun theme of the bag, while beads and buttons add the perfect decorative touches. The details really make the bag, so spend time choosing beads, buttons and fabrics.

Using fusible web makes the cupcake appliqué on this bag really easy. A scattering of seed beads look like 'hundreds and thousands' on the icing, while a pink button is the cherry on top.

## you will need ...

- ✿ two pieces of thick felt in grey 20.3 x 25.4cm (8 x 10in) each

- ✿ craft felt in beige and white about 10.2 x 6.3cm (4 x 2½in) each

- ✿ pink spotted cotton fabric 10.2 x 6.3cm (4 x 2½in)

- ✿ fusible web

- ✿ ready-made D-shaped handles in pink and white stripe

- ✿ pale pink ribbon 1cm (⅜in) wide x 25.4cm (10in)

- ✿ pink and white striped pre-ruffled ribbon 61cm (24in) long

- ✿ embroidery cotton (floss) in colours to match fabrics

- ✿ seed beads in various colours

- ✿ one red button and ten white ones

**1** The finished size of the bag is 18 x 23cm (7 x 9in). Enlarge the template to full size and make a paper template for the bag shape. Use the template to cut out two pieces of thick grey felt. Use the cupcake templates to trace the three shapes on to fusible web. Iron on to the back of the relevant fabrics (white felt for the icing, beige felt for the cake, pink spotted cotton for the case).

**2** Cut out the shapes and position on to the front of one of the grey felt pieces. Iron to fuse in place. Use a running stitch in matching embroidery cotton to stitch around the edges of the shapes and to make the stripes on the case. Sew a few multicoloured seed beads on to the icing and stitch a red button on the top like a cherry.

**3** Along the top edge of the bag, sew a row of small white buttons using pink thread. Place the front and back panels of the bag together, with the length of ruffled pink and white striped ribbon between them. Pin all around the curved edge and then stitch together with a 6mm (¼in) seam. Alternatively, you could make your own ruffle – see the tip below.

**4** Cut four 6.3cm (2½in) lengths of 1cm (⅜in) wide pale pink ribbon and thread through the holes at the bottom of the plastic handles. Secure the handles in place by stitching two ribbons at the top of the bag front and two at the back.

If making your own ruffle ribbon start with a length of flat ribbon about 1.5m (1½yd) long. Using a strong thread, work a running stitch along the length of the ribbon, about 6mm (¼in) in from one edge. Gather the ribbon by pulling on this thread, until the ruffle is long enough to go around the outside of the bag.

*techniques* basic tools... preparing for work... sewing techniques... attaching beads... attaching buttons... templates

cupcake bag 81

techniques

# basic tools

Each project in the book has its own You Will Need list, detailing the specific materials and equipment required to make it, however, you will also need some general supplies, as listed below.

## Sewing Tools

- fabric markers and pencils
- needles, pins and safety pins
- scissors (fabric and embroidery)
- tape measure
- sewing and embroidery threads
- sewing machine
- iron
- fusible web

## Papercraft Tools

- craft knife, metal ruler and cutting mat
- craft glue and double-sided tape
- tracing paper
- pair of compasses
- dimensional fluid
- circle punches in small and medium
- die-cutting system
- embossing folder
- bone folder (optional)

## Jewellery Tools

- jump rings
- findings (earring wires, necklace fastenings)
- round-nose and long-nose pliers

## Soap Making Tools

- soap moulds
- rubbing alcohol in spray bottle
- microwave-safe glass measuring cup
- soap thermometer
- small saucepan

## Knitting Tools

- knitting needles
- double-pointed needles
- stitch marker
- darning needle
- crochet hook

## Needle Felting Tools

- foam work surface
- felting needles size 36–38

# preparing for work

Before you start work on your selected project, there are a few things you will need to prepare in advance, which are outlined in this section.

## Gather your tools and materials

Check the project 'you will need' list and read through the project instructions before you begin, to make sure you have all tools and materials to hand. Check the list of basic tools opposite too, to see what other general equipment you might need.

## Using templates

All templates should be used at the size given unless stated otherwise. Most are printed actual size, but a few need to be enlarged on a photocopier at the percentage given. Trace around the template shape, pin the tracing on the fabric and cut out the shape. When tracing shapes on to fusible web,

remember that the finished image will be reversed, so flip the tracing over before copying it on to the fusible web.

## Preparing patterns

If you need to make a paper template as a pattern, you can pin it on to the fabric and then either cut it out around the template or use a fabric pen or pencil to draw around the template before cutting it out.

## Pinning patterns

General dressmakers' pins are suitable for most fabrics, although silks and fine cottons should be pinned with fine pins, such as bridal or lace pins. Pin the straight grain first (the least stretchy direction), and then

pin around the pattern piece, diagonally at the corners and vertical to the pattern edge.

# sewing techniques

The techniques needed for creating the fabric projects in the book are given in this section. Some of these techniques may also be needed for the other projects.

## Preparing fabric

Prepare your fabrics by pre-washing them before use in mild detergent to check that the colours do not run and to allow for any shrinkage that might occur. Pre-wash cotton lining or interfacings too. For delicate fabrics where washing is best avoided, such as silk and wool, gently tighten the fibres and help prevent shrinkage by hovering a steam iron 3–4cm (1¼ –1¾in) above the cloth.

## Cutting fabric

It is important when cutting out to have a clean, large flat surface to work on and to always cut away from yourself.

## Using scissors

Ensure that your fabric shears are sharp. To cut accurately, position your fabric to the left of the shears (or to the right if you are left-handed) and follow the edge of the pattern line, taking long strokes for straight edges and shorter strokes for curved areas.

## Using a rotary cutter

A rotary cutter has a very sharp blade and is perfect for cutting out fabric into strips or squares, for patchwork for example. Cut away from the body when using a rotary cutter. Cover the blade when not in use. The same principles apply when using a craft knife to cut paper and card.

**1** Position a ruler firmly on top of your fabric and square off any uneven ends.

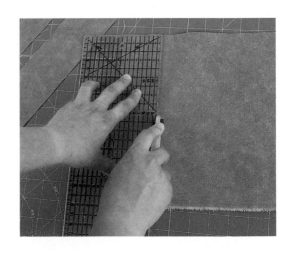

**2** Turn your cutting mat around 180 degrees and line up the relevant mark on the ruler, e.g., 6.5cm (2½in) if 5cm (2in) is the finished size required (allowing for the seam allowance when sewing the fabric squares together). Line up your rotary cutter against the ruler's edge and cut.

## Marking fabrics

There are many ways to mark designs on to fabrics before stitching and two are described here.

## Using a fade-away pen

Any marks made with a fade-away pen will disappear in time (air-soluble) or with a little water (water-soluble). Use the pen to draw the line you want to follow with stitching. Once stitched, dab a little water on to remove water-soluble marks.

## Using a fabric pencil or tailor's chalk

Any marks made with a fabric pencil or tailors' chalk will rub off when no longer needed. Draw the line or pattern with the pencil and take care not to rub it out as you stitch. Once the stitching is complete, rub the pencil marks to remove.

## Sewing by hand

The projects in this book use a variety of hand stitches for functional and decorative work. When sewing by hand choose a needle that matches the thickness of the thread you are using, so the thread passes easily through the fabric. You will need general hand sewing needles, a beading needle and a darning needle for finishing off knitted projects. All stitches can be started with a knot on the back of the work and finished off neatly at the back, usually with some tiny backstitches.

## Backstitch

Backstitch is often worked on its own for lettering or to add detail and can be worked to follow a design line.

Bring the needle and thread up to the front of the work and take a backward stitch, taking the needle and thread through to the back. Bring the needle up to the front again, a little way ahead of the first stitch, and back down into the point where the first stitch began. Repeat along the line to be stitched.

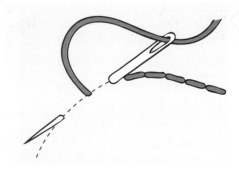

## Blanket stitch

This stitch can be used to create a decorative edging, especially around appliqué motifs.

Working from left to right (or the opposite direction if left-handed), bring the needle and thread up from the back of the fabric to the front, a little way in from the edge, the distance depending on the size of stitches you want. Leave the loose thread running down over the edge or at

right angles to it. Take the threaded end over the loose end and insert the needle a little way along, the same distance from the edge as before. Pass the needle through the loop of thread and pull up the thread so it fits snugly along the edge. Repeat along the edge to be stitched.

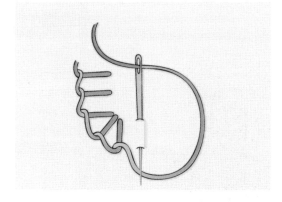

## Buttonhole stitch

If making buttonholes in fabric the neatest effect will be obtained using a sewing machine. If working by hand, this stitch is worked in the same way as blanket stitch, above, but with the stitches worked closely side by side.

For wool projects a buttonhole loop can be used to secure a button, as for the Magic Mitten Gloves. Stitch a small loop using two strands of yarn and then work buttonhole stitch evenly and snugly over and all along the loop using the same stitch formation as blanket stitch. Work the stitches tightly to fill the length of the loop.

## Catch stitch

This little stitch is used to sew one piece of fabric to another. Simply tie a knot in the thread and bring the needle up from the back of the work near the join of the

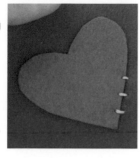

two fabrics. Make a small stitch that overlaps the two fabrics in a straight line and push the needle through to the back. Bring the needle up again a little way away and repeat.

## French knot

This is a decorative little knot. Bring the needle from the back to the front of the work and wind the thread (or wool yarn) twice round the

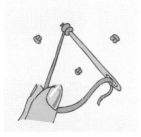

needle. Holding the thread taut, pull the needle through the twists bringing the thread (or yarn) through too. This creates the knot. For a bigger knot twist the thread (or yarn) round the needle more times or once only for a smaller knot.

## Running stitch

This very simple stitch, sometimes called quilting stitch, creates a line of dashes. It can be worked with embroidery cotton or wool yarn. Thread a needle with the thread you want to use (this will need to be a bigger tapestry or darning needle if using wool) and insert it from the back of the work through to the front where you want the stitch to start. Make small, regularly spaced stitches along the line.

## Slipstitch

This stitch is used for hems, to close gaps in seams, to attach pockets and so on – anywhere you do not want the stitches to show too much.

Work small, neat stitches in a thread that matches the fabric colour, so that the stitches are almost invisible. Work from right to left (if right-handed), picking up a tiny piece of the fabric from one seam edge with the needle. Insert the needle into the other seam fold, moving it along inside the fold about 3mm (⅛in). Push the needle out into the seam again and repeat.

## Attaching beads

Whether large or small, beads look fantastic on many projects. Seed beads are small round beads with a hole in the centre, bugle beads are long cylinders of glass with a hole along the centre and sequins are flat disks, usually made from metal foil or plastic. If you're using tiny seed beads, use a very fine beading needle, to fit through the hole in the bead.

### Single beads

To stitch on a bead, thread a beading needle with fine thread in the same colour as the bead and tie a knot at the end. Push the needle through the fabric from back to front at the point you want the bead to be. Thread the bead on to the needle and pull the thread through, then push the needle back through the same point it entered and secure the thread, or continue on to the next bead.

To sew a line of bugle beads, bring the needle and thread up to the front of the fabric at the start of the line, thread on as many bugles as are needed to cover the line and take the thread back down at the end of the line and secure at the back.

### Sequins

The Felt Flower Necklace and the Birthday Bunting use sequins and beads.

To sew on a single sequin, stitch through the hole three times, angling the stitches out from the centre each time. Secure the thread at the back with a few tiny stitches.

To add a sequin with a bead in the centre, push the threaded needle up though one of the sequin holes, through the seed bead and then back down through the other hole in the sequin, missing the bead this time. Secure the thread at the back.

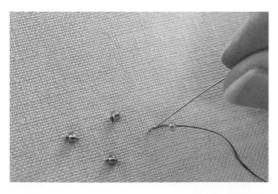

## Attaching buttons

Buttons are not only functional but also very decorative and they have been used on the Button Bangle, Dishy Delight and the Cupcake Bag. Use flat buttons for these projects, with two or four holes. Thread used to sew on buttons can match the button or contrast with it for more impact. Buttons can be sewn in position using either straight stitches or in a cross shape.

To sew on a button, make a stitch where the button is to be positioned. Hold the button a little away from the fabric and sew through the button holes into the fabric or base material at least three times. Lift the button away from the fabric and wind the thread around the stitches. Take the needle and thread through to the back and finish off securely.

## Appliqué

Appliqué is the name for the technique of attaching fabric shapes to other fabrics and the easiest way to do this is with a product called fusible web. This has various trade names, including Bondaweb, WonderWeb, Wonder Under and Vliesofix. It comes in a roll or in pre-cut pieces and looks like paper. One side can be drawn on (so you can trace the shape you want) and the other has a thin membrane of glue that melts when heated by an iron, so allowing two fabrics to be glued together. Designs traced on to fusible web will come out in reverse, so if you don't want this then you will need to flip the tracing first. Be careful to iron only the paper side, otherwise the glue will stick to your iron. If this happens, use an iron cleaner to remove it.

## Using fusible web – method 1

**1** Use a hot iron to fuse the fusible web on to the back of the fabric you wish to appliqué. Pin the template to the front of the backed fabric and cut out the shape. Straight scissors can be used.

**2** Carefully peel the backing paper away, position the motif on the base fabric and press with a hot iron for several seconds to fuse it in position.

## Using fusible web – method 2

**1** Trace the shape you want on to the paper side of the fusible web. Cut out roughly around this shape and then iron it on to the back of the fabric you wish to appliqué.

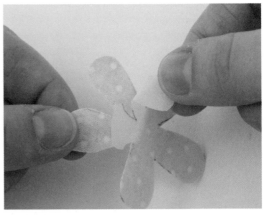

**2** Carefully cut out the shape and peel off the paper backing. Place the shape on to the base fabric and use a medium to hot iron for several seconds to fuse it in position.

*tip* When using a fusible web, always check that the fabric you plan to use can be ironed without shrivelling or melting!

# Using a sewing machine

A sewing machine produces a consistent and strong stitch and will allow you to complete projects faster. It is worth the investment if you intend doing a lot of sewing. Take some time to read your sewing machine manual and become familiar with the functions before you begin.

## Presser feet

The presser foot holds the fabric firmly against the needle plate while the stitch is formed. It is important to use the correct presser foot for the stitch you are using and to test your tension on a scrap of fabric before you begin. Here are a few presser feet that you will find useful.

• General-purpose foot (A) – for general sewing, utility and embroidery stitches on ordinary fabrics.
• Zipper foot (B) – a narrower foot for sewing in zips and piping. The needle can be adjusted to sew on either side.

• Clear view foot (C) – essential for accurate work as it allows you to see where you are stitching. It can be made from clear fabric or cut away. This foot is ideal for working on bulky fabrics and for machine appliqué.

## Machine needles

Use an appropriate machine needle for your work and change it frequently – immediately if damaged or bent. It is handy to keep a selection of the most popular needle sizes.

• Size 70 (9) – for silks and fine cottons (A).
• Size 100 (16) – for leather (B).
• Size 90 (14) – for denims, canvas and heavyweight linens (C).

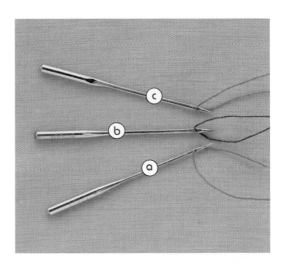

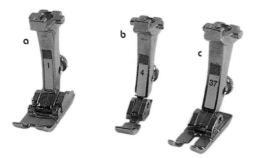

## Preparing for machine sewing

Before you begin to stitch, prepare your material. Pinning and tacking (basting) are useful ways of ensuring your fabric is lined up and stays in the correct place when machine sewing.

**Tacking (basting)** – Tacking fabrics together will ensure that they stay in place as you sew them. Using a thin thread, sew the fabrics together by hand with large running stitches. When you reach the end of the fabric, do not secure the thread with a knot but leave a long tail. When it is time to remove tacking, use an unpicker tool or a pin to pull out the stitches.

**Pinning** – You can use pins to sew two fabrics together by machine without tacking (basting). Place the fabrics together, edge to edge. Insert the pins at right angles to the edges of the fabrics, leaving a small gap between the pins. Stitch slowly over the pins – the needle will slip over each pin without bending them. Remove the pins when stitching is complete.

## Machine stitches

The type of machine you have will determine the range of stitches available to you. Listed here are the main stitches that you will need to use on your sewing machine to complete the projects in this book.

**Straight stitch (A)** – This stitch is the most widely used to join two pieces of fabric together. It can be used for sewing seams and topstitching. For ordinary fabric, set your stitch length to 3mm (⅛in) for tidy, even stitches. For fine fabrics use a shorter stitch length, and increase the stitch length for heavier fabrics. Topstitching is a short straight stitch normally sewn about 3mm (⅛in) from the edge of a seam to keep it flat and neat.

**Zigzag (B)** – This is a versatile stitch, used to neaten seams and edges, as a decorative edge and to hold appliqué motifs in place. To neaten seams, it is best to set your zigzag stitch to 2mm (³/₃₂in) in width and length. When using for appliqué, set your zigzag to 2mm (³/₃₂in) and between 0.5 and 1mm (³/₃₂–¹/₁₆in) in length.

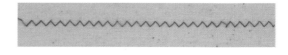

## Sewing a seam by machine

One of the most basic tasks in any sewing project is sewing a seam. The following techniques use a 1.5cm (½in) seam allowance, which can be adjusted for each project as necessary.

Tack (baste) or pin the seam across the seam line, with the right sides of your fabric together.

Place your fabric under the presser foot so that the edge of the seam is next to the 1.5cm (½in) line on the needle plate and the fabric is 6mm (¼in) behind the needle. Use the hand wheel to take the needle down into the fabric, and then begin to sew. Sew at a comfortable speed, guiding the fabric along the 1.5cm (½in) line on the needle plate.

Finished seams can be neatened to prevent them from fraying and weakening. A small, narrow machine zigzag along the raw edges is one of the fastest – try different stitch lengths and widths to find which suits the fabric best. Trim the seam to 6mm (¼in) and zigzag both edges together.

### Turning corners
This is a basic skill that is essential when sewing more than one side of a project. Stitch down the first length, leaving a 1.5cm (½in) seam allowance. Slow down as you approach the corner and use the hand wheel to complete the last few stitches. Stop 1.5cm (½in) from the edge, with the needle in the fabric. Lift the presser foot and turn the fabric around so the next seam is lined up with the guideline on the needle plate. Lower the presser foot and continue to sew.

## Inserting a zip
While it is possible to hand stitch a zip in position, a machine-sewn zip will be more secure and hard wearing. You will need to fit a zipper foot to the machine to enable you to sew as close to the zip teeth as possible, but be careful not to sew over the teeth, which can break the needle.

Tack (baste) the zip in place and allow 1.5cm (½in) seam allowances. Fold under the first piece of fabric by 1.5cm (½in) and pin it to the zip. The folded edge should be close to the teeth but allow the zip to be unfastened. Machine sew down the edge about 3mm (⅛in) from the fold. Sew the second piece of fabric to the zip the same way.

*tip* Sew with the zip open. Stop sewing at the pull with the needle down in the fabric, draw the pull past and continue stitching.

# knitting techniques

This section will be very useful to those new to knitting, helping you to work the projects in the book. It is best to read these pages before you start working on a project.

## Knitting gauge

The gauge or tension is the number of stitches and rows needed to knit 2.5cm (1in). Most knitting and crochet projects recommend that you knit a gauge square or swatch before starting the project in order to stitch the project to the correct size and fit. The gauge is given over 10.2cm (4in) at the start of a project. To check your gauge, knit a square at least 15.2cm (6in), using the stated yarn, needle size and stitch. Measure the square to check your

gauge is correct (in the middle, not the edges, which may be distorted). If it isn't, you will need to knit tighter or looser.

## Pattern sizes

Knitting instructions normally describe several sizes simultaneously, giving alternate sizes in square brackets. For example, cast on 45 [51: 57] sts. So if you want to knit the smallest size choose the first number each time, i.e., 45. If you want to knit the largest size choose the last number each time, i.e., 57.

## Knitting abbreviations

Abbreviations are used in knitting patterns to shorten commonly used terms so that the instructions are easier to read and a manageable length. The following is a list of the abbreviations you need to make the projects in this book. The tinted panel opposite lists the most common differences in US and UK knitting terms.

approx ........ approximately
beg ............. beginning
cm .............. centimetre(s)
cont ........... continue
dec(s) ........ decrease/decreasing
DK ............. double knitting
dpn ............ double-pointed needles
foll ............. following
g ............... gram(s)
inc ............. increase(s)/increasing
in(s) .......... Inch(es)
k ................ knit
k2tog ......... knit 2 stitches together (1 stitch
.................. decreased)
k3tog ......... knit 3 stitches together (2 stitches
.................. decreased)
k2tog tbl ..... knit 2 stitches together through back of
.................. loops (1 stitch decreased)
kf&b ........... knit into front and back of stitch
.................. (1 stitch increased)
m ............... metre(s)
mm ............ millimetres
M1 ............. make one (increase 1 stitch)
oz .............. ounces
p ............... purl
patt(s) ........ pattern(s)
pfb ............. purl into front and back of stitch (to
.................. increase by 1 stitch)
p2tog ........ purl 2 stitches together
.................. (1 stitch decreased)
p3tog ........ purl 3 stitches together
.................. (2 stitches decreased)
rem ............ remain/remaining
rep(s) ........ repeat(s)

RS .............. right side
sl ............... slip
ss .............. slip stitch
ssk ............. slip 2 stitches one at a time, knit
.................. 2 slipped stitches together
.................. (1 stitch decreased)
st st ........... stockinette (stocking) stitch
.................. (1 row k, 1 row p)
st(s) .......... stitch(es)
tbl .............. through back of loop
tog ............ together
WS ............. wrong side
yd(s) ......... yards(s)
yo .............. yarn over
* ............... repeat directions following * as many
times as indicated or to end of row
[ ] .............. instructions in square brackets refer to
larger sizes
( ) .............. repeat instructions in round brackets
the number of times

## knitting terms...

| US term | UK term |
| --- | --- |
| stockinette stitch | stocking stitch |
| reverse stockinette stitch | reverse stocking stitch |
| seed stitch | moss stitch |
| moss stitch | double moss stitch or seed stitch |
| bind off | cast off |
| gauge | tension |

## Casting on

To begin knitting, you need to work a foundation row of stitches and this is called casting on. There are several ways to cast on stitches and a cable cast-on method is described here.

### Cable cast-on method

This gives a neat, firm edge that is also elastic making it perfect as an edging for rib stitch. It is also used to cast on stitches in the middle of a row, sometimes called picking up stitches.

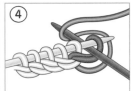

**1** Take two needles and make a slip knot about 15cm (6in) from the end of the yarn on one needle. Hold this needle in your left hand. Insert the right-hand needle knitwise into the loop on the left-hand needle and wrap the yarn around the tip.

**2** Pull the yarn through the loop to make a stitch but do not drop the stitch off the left-hand needle.

**3** Slip the new stitch on to the left-hand needle by inserting the left-hand needle into the front of the loop from right to left. You will now have two stitches on the left-hand needle.

**4** Insert the right-hand needle between the two stitches on the left-hand needle and wrap the yarn around the tip. Pull the yarn back through between the two stitches and place it on the left-hand needle, as in step 3. Repeat until you have cast on the required number of stitches.

**To cast on extra stitches mid row** – Work step 4 only, working the first stitch between the next two stitches already on the left-hand needle.

## Using a stitch marker

Stitch markers are used to mark your place in a row of knitting and are especially useful in circular knitting, or knitting in the round, where it is not obvious where the circle begins and ends. They are usually made of plastic or metal and are slipped on to the knitting needle.

# Knit stitch (k)

This is the simplest stitch of all. Each stitch is created with a four-step process. Hold the yarn at the back of the work – this is the side facing away from you.

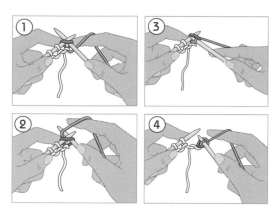

**1** Place the needle with the cast-on stitches in your left hand, insert the right-hand needle into the front of the first stitch on the left hand needle from left to right.

**2** Take the yarn around and under the point of the right-hand needle.

**3** Draw the new loop on the right-hand needle through the stitch on the left-hand needle.

**4** Slide the stitch off the left-hand needle. This has formed one knit stitch on the right-hand needle.

Repeat until all stitches on the left-hand needle have been transferred to the right-hand needle. This is the end of the row. Swap the right-hand needle into your left hand and begin the next row in exactly the same way.

## Knit stitch – continental method

In this method the right-hand needle moves to catch the yarn; the yarn is held at the back of the work (the side facing away from you) and is released by the index finger of the left hand.

**1** Hold the needle with the cast on stitches in your left hand and the yarn over your left index finger. Insert the right-hand needle into the front of the stitch from left to right.

**2** Move the right-hand needle down and across the back of the yarn. (Continued overleaf.)

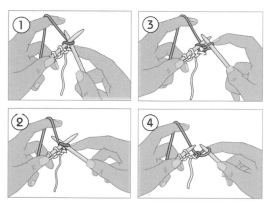

**3** Pull the new loop on the right-hand needle through the stitch on the left-hand needle, using the right index finger to hold the new loop if needed.

**4** Slip the stitch off the left-hand needle. One knit stitch is completed.

## Purl stitch (p)

This is the reverse of knit stitch. Hold the yarn at the front of the work – this is the side facing you.

**1** Place the needle with the cast-on stitches in your left hand, insert the right-hand needle into the front of the first stitch on the left-hand needle from right to left.

**2** Take the yarn over and around the point of the right-hand needle.

**3** Draw the new loop on the right-hand needle through the stitch on the left-hand needle.

**4** Slide the stitch off the left-hand needle. This has formed one purl stitch on the right-hand needle. Repeat these four steps to the end of the row.

## Purl stitch – continental method

Hold the yarn in the left hand, at the front of the work (the side facing you).

**1** Hold the needle with the cast on stitches in your left hand and insert the right-hand needle into the front of the stitch from right to left, keeping the yarn at the front of the work.

**2** Move the right-hand needle from right to left behind the yarn and then from left to right in front

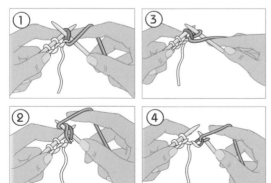

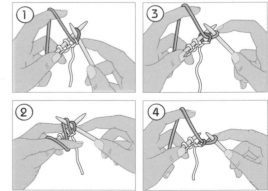

of the yarn. Pull your left index finger down in front of the work to keep the yarn taut.

**3** Pull the new loop on the right-hand needle through the stitch on the left-hand needle, using the right index finger to hold the new loop if needed.

**4** Slip the stitch off the left-hand needle. Return the left index finger to its position above the needle. One stitch is completed.

## Stockinette stitch (st st)

Stockinette or stocking stitch is formed by working alternate knit and purl rows. The knit rows are the right side of the fabric and the purl rows are the wrong side. Instructions for stockinette stitch in knitting patterns can be written as follows:

Row 1 RS Knit
Row 2 Purl
Or alternatively: Work in st st (1 row k, 1 row p), beg with a k row.

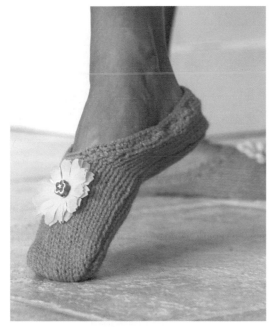

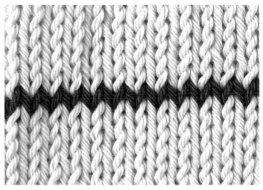

*tip* To work a row of stockinette stitch you will need yarn measuring four times the width of the knitting.

## Knitting in the round

Knitting in the round is a method where a tube of knitting is formed rather than a flat piece, so the knitting is worked in rounds, not rows. This can be done by using a circular needle or double-pointed needles. When you reach the end of a round you simply carry on knitting without turning the needles. Double-pointed needles are shorter than standard needles and are easier to handle than a circular needle when you only have a few stitches to work on or when working in the round.

**1** Cast on normally, distributing the stitches evenly over three double-pointed needles.

**2** Continue knitting round, transferring the stitches along each needle so you have an equal number of stitches on each needle. You may want to place a stitch marker at the beginning of the round.

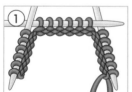

## Changing yarn colour

Knitting with different colours is part of the fun when creating garments, accessories and toys so you need to know how to join in a new yarn colour.

**1** Insert the tip of the right-hand needle into the next stitch, place the cut end of the new colour over the old colour and over the tip of the right-hand needle. Take the working end of the new colour and knit the next stitch, pulling the cut end off the needle over the working end as the stitch is formed so it is not knitted in. Hold the cut end down against the back of the work.

**2** Once you've joined in all the colours that you need across the row, on the return row twist the yarns to join the blocks of colour together. When you change colour, always pick up the new colour from under the old yarn.

## Increasing stitches

Increasing stitches is a way of shaping the knitting and there are several methods. Those described here can be used for the projects in this book, including the Magic Mitten Gloves.

### Make 1 (M1) – twist M1 to the left

This increase is used for shaping the thumb gusset on the mitten gloves. Use both the right- and left-twisting versions for a neat finish to the gusset. The new stitch is made between two existing stitches using the horizontal thread that lies between the stitches.

**1** Knit to the point where the increase is to be made. Insert the tip of the left-hand needle under the running thread from front to back.

**2** Knit this loop through the back to twist it. By twisting it you prevent a hole appearing where the made stitch is.

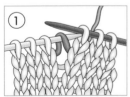 

### Make 1 (M1) – twist M1 to the right

**1** Knit to the point where the increase is to be made. Insert the tip of the left-hand needle under the running thread from back to front.

**2** Knit this loop through the front to twist it.

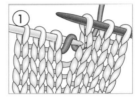 

### Knit into front and back (Kf&b)

An easy way to increase one stitch is by working into the front and back of the same stitch.

Knit into the front of the stitch as usual. Do not slip the stitch off the left-hand needle but knit into it again through the back of the loop, and then slip the original stitch off the left-hand needle. You can make a stitch on a purl row in the same way but purling into the front and back of the stitch (pfb).

## Decreasing stitches

As well as being able to increase stitches you will need to be able to decrease stitches for shaping. Stitches can be decreased singly or by several at once. Several methods are described here.

### Decreasing one stitch – knit 2 together (K2tog)

Knit to where the decrease is to be, insert the right-hand needle (as though to knit) through the next two stitches and knit them together as one stitch.

### Decreasing one stitch – purl 2 together (P2tog)

Purl to where the decrease is to be, insert the right-hand needle (as though to purl) through the next two stitches and purl them together as one stitch.

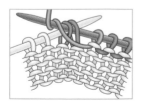

### Decreasing one stitch – slip 2 stitches knitwise (ssk or k2tog tbl)

**1** Slip two stitches knitwise one at a time from the left-hand needle to the right-hand needle (they will be twisted).

**2** Insert the left-hand needle from left to right through the fronts and knit together as one stitch (k2tog tbl).

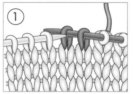 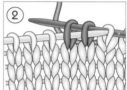

### Decreasing one stitch – slip 2 stitches purlwise (ssp or p2tog tbl)

**1** Slip two stitches knitwise, one at a time, from the left-hand needle to the right-hand needle (they will be twisted). Pass these two stitches back to the left-hand needle in this twisted way.

**2** Purl together through the back loops (p2togtbl).

## Decreasing two stitches at once

There are various ways of doing this.

• K3tog: Work as k2tog, but knit three stitches together instead of two.

• P3tog: Work as p2tog, but purl three stitches together instead of two.

• K3tog tbl: Work as ssk (or k2tog tbl), but slip three stitches instead of two and knit them together.

• P3tog tbl: Work as ssp, but slip three stitches instead of two and purl them together through the backs of the loops.

## Binding off

Binding off (casting off) links and secures stitches together so that the knitting cannot unravel when completed. Binding off is normally done following the stitch sequence, so a knit stitch is bound off knitwise and a purl stitch purlwise. Don't bind off too tightly as this may pull the fabric in. To bind off on a purl row, follow the Bind Off Knitwise steps but purl the stitches instead of knitting them.

## Bind off knitwise

**1** Knit the first two stitches. Insert the point of the left-hand needle into the front of the first stitch on the right-hand needle.

**2** Lift the first stitch on the right-hand needle over the second stitch and off the needle. One stitch is left on the right-hand needle.

**3** Knit the next stitch on the left-hand needle, so there are again two stitches on the right-hand needle. Lift the first stitch on the right-hand needle over the second stitch, as in step 2. Repeat this until one stitch is left on the right-hand needle. Cut the yarn (leaving a length long enough to sew in) and pass the end through the last stitch. Slip the stitch off the needle and pull the yarn end to tighten it.

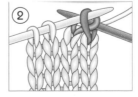

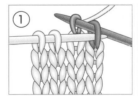

## Darning in ends

You will have some loose ends from casting on, binding off and changing colours and these can be woven into the knitting to secure them and create a neat look. Thread the loose end through a large-eyed tapestry or darning needle and pass the needle through the 'bumps' of the stitches on the back of the work for about 5cm (2in) and then snip off excess yarn.

## Sewing up

There are different methods for seaming or sewing your knitted pieces together depending on the finish you want to achieve. If possible, sew up your items with the same yarn you used to knit them. If the yarn is very thick, highly textured or breaks easily, use a plain yarn in a matching colour.

## Seaming with overcasting

Overcasting is a useful method of joining knitted pieces as it creates a narrow, flat seam. It is usually worked from the wrong side. Pin the pieces to be joined with their right sides together, matching the stitches exactly. Thread a tapestry or darning needle with yarn about 45cm (18in) long and join the yarn securely at the edge of the two seams. Work along the seam taking the needle under the strands at the edge of the seam, between the matched 'bumps', from back to front. Tighten the yarn gently over the knitted edge after each stitch, keeping the tension of each stitch the same.

## Knitting mittens and gloves

Mittens are easy to knit and a great introduction to knitting gloves. The information here will help you when you are knitting the Magic Mitten Gloves.

## Thumb gusset

The thumb on each hand is not added on to the side but angled more towards the palm. So stitches have to be added to accommodate the thumb and this is called the thumb gusset. These stitches are made by working an M1 (make one) on each side of two stitches. Imagine the stitches on your needle divided into two; one half is for the back of the mitten and the other half is for the palm. The first increase is made before the first of the palm stitches and the second after two of the palm stitches.

## Thumb

The thumb is worked on the stitches of the thumb gusset plus some extra stitches to fit around the back of the thumb, which need to be cast on using the cable cast-on method. The thumb is shaped at the top to make a rounded end.

The thumb seam is joined for the next bit of knitting. Because the two stitches at the beginning of the thumb gusset (between the increases) were used to knit the thumb, they need to be replaced to get back to the original number of stitches at the wrist. Two stitches are picked up across the cast-on edge of the thumb; one each side of the seam. The mitten is knitted straight to the top shaping; this is simple shaping to give the mitten a rounded finish.

## Fingers

Each finger is knitted using some of the stitches already on the needles and some extra stitches that are cast on. The second, third and fourth finger all pick up stitches from the base of the previous finger. The seam of the fourth finger is also the side seam, so no stitches are cast on here. The extra stitches are all picked up along the base of the third finger – four stitches instead of the usual two.

When you re-join the yarn to pick up stitches at the base of the thumb or finger, leave a long end of yarn for sewing in. These joins must be sewn securely. You can also use these ends to sew up any holes that might appear around the base of the fingers or thumb.

# crochet techniques

Crochet is a simple technique to learn and a great way to create projects or add embellishment to knitted projects, such as the Ballerina Slippers.

## Crochet abbreviations and conversions

Abbreviations are used in crochet patterns to shorten commonly used terms so that the instructions are easier to read and a manageable length. You should be aware that crochet terms in the US are different from those in the UK. This can be confusing as the same terms are used to refer to different stitches under each system. The list here gives abbreviations and a translation of US terms to UK terms.

| US term | UK term |
|---|---|
| slip stitch | single crochet |
| single crochet (sc) | double crochet |
| half double crochet (hdc) | half treble |
| double crochet | treble |
| treble crochet | double treble |
| double treble crochet | treble treble |

## Crochet hook sizes

British and international crocheters use the metric system for crochet hook sizes, whereas the US has its own system. The crochet hook size is usually selected based on the size of yarn being used.

| US size | UK size | | |
|---|---|---|---|
| B 1 | 2.5mm | H 8 | 5mm |
| C 2 | 2.75mm | I 9 | 5.5mm |
| D 3 | 3.25mm | J 10 | 6mm |
| E 4 | 3.5mm | K 10½ | 6.5mm |
| F 5 | 3.75mm | L 11 | 8mm |
| G 6 | 4mm | M/N 13 | 9mm |
| 7 | 4.5mm | N/P 15 | 10mm |
| | | P/Q | 15mm |

## Slip knot

Create a loop with the yarn, making sure that the tail of the yarn is dangling behind the loop. Insert the crochet hook through the loop, moving under the tail and back out of the loop. Grab the tail with the hook and pull to create the slip knot on the crochet hook.

## Chain stitch (ch)

There are various ways that chain stitch can be used. It can be worked as a single stitch, or in a row to form a long chain, or be joined into a circle.

Tie a slip knot in the working end of your yarn and place the loop on the crochet hook. Wrap the yarn clockwise over the hook and then pull the yarn through the loop on the hook to form a fresh loop. This is one chain stitch. Repeat the process until you have as many chain stitches as needed.

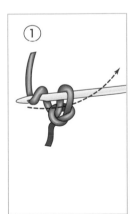

## Single crochet (sc)

The single crochet stitch is the shortest of the crochet stitches. To make the stitch, insert your hook under the top two strands of the stitch beneath (or, if you're working into the foundation row, insert the hook into the centre of the chain stitch). Wrap the yarn over the hook and pull the yarn through. Then wrap the yarn over the hook again and pull it through both the loops on the hook. This forms one single crochet stitch.

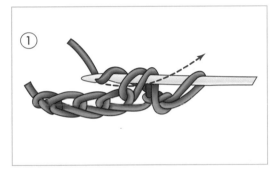

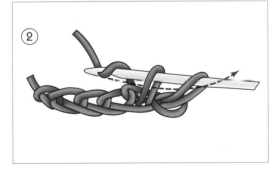

# papercraft techniques

There are many techniques used to create projects from paper and card but the Retro Cards, Cake Slice and Funky Flowers projects in this book only use the following ones.

## Making a card blank

Greetings card blanks can be bought ready-made but it's so easy to make your own, which will also give you a much wider choice of card colour, weight and texture. Choose your card colour and a weight heavy enough so the card will stand upright.

**1** Decide on the size of finished card you need and cut a piece of card this height and twice the width. Make two pencil marks halfway along the width, at the top and bottom, where you want the card to fold. Score a line between these marks using an empty ballpoint pen or a scoring tool.

**2** Use both hands to neatly fold the card along the score line, using a bone folder or the back of a metal spoon to create a firm crease.

## Curling paper

Paper may be curled in several ways, tightly or loosely, depending on its weight and the size of the piece. Paper, like fabric, has a definite grain, and it is much easier to curl it with the grain rather than against it. To find the grain, take a sample of the paper and tear it in half. If it leaves a ragged edge and is difficult to control, you are tearing against the grain. If it tears easily, with a smooth line, you are tearing with the grain.

## Curling light/medium-weight strips

To tightly curl narrow strips of lightweight to medium-weight paper and lightweight card, hold firmly in one hand and pull the paper over the closed blades of a pair of scissors. Don't pull thin paper too hard or it will tear.

## Curling heavier paper and card

Find the grain of the paper first and then roll it tightly, with the grain, around a pencil. Hold in place for a few seconds to keep the shape.

## Rolling paper

To give paper a gently rolled effect, hold it firmly in one hand and pull along the length between finger and thumb several times. It can then be curved into whatever shape you need, and will fold into gentle waves with ease.

*tip*
Another way to find the grain of paper or card, is to fold it vertically and then horizontally. The fold that is straight and smooth is along the grain; the fold that is a little more bumpy and uneven is going against the grain.

## Making tabbed walls

Using tabbed walls is the easiest way to make
a shape three-dimensional, such as the Cake
Slice project. A paper or card strip is snipped into
tabs and scored along one or both sides. These
can then be manipulated to follow curves, circles
and other shapes. Tabs can then be glued to
the shape to create a side, or glued to join two
shapes if tabbed on both sides.

**1** Cut the strip to the width and length required.
Draw a 1–1.5cm (³⁄₈–⁵⁄₈in) deep border along one
or both sides. Snip carefully along the wall as far
as the border, approximately every 1.5cm (⁵⁄₈in).

**2** Place the wall right side up on a cutting mat.
Score along the border with the wrong side of a
craft knife blade. Fold under the tabs.

**3** To attach the wall to a curved shape, curl it
between finger and thumb to make it pliable.
Spread glue on the tabs and curve the wall around
your shape, matching the wall to the profile of the
shape as precisely as possible. Press down the
tabs, trim the wall to size and finally, glue and
overlap the ends.

# templates

Use the templates at the size shown unless otherwise stated. If they need to be enlarged to full size use a photocopier, entering the enlargement percentage given. For further information on templates see Using Templates in the techniques section.

## felt flower necklace

actual size

necklace flower

ring flower

ring flower

necklace flower

## ipod sweater

actual size

dishy delight

actual size

large flower for
centre of dish

small flower for
corners of dish

birdie album

actual size

retro cards

actual size

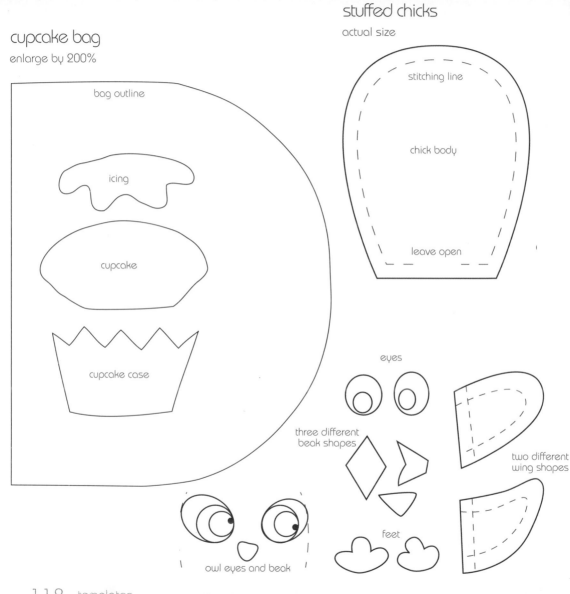

## cupcake bag
enlarge by 200%

bag outline

icing

cupcake

cupcake case

## stuffed chicks
actual size

stitching line

chick body

leave open

eyes

three different
beak shapes

two different
wing shapes

feet

owl eyes and beak

# cake slice
enlarge by 200%

# birthday bunting
enlarge by 200%

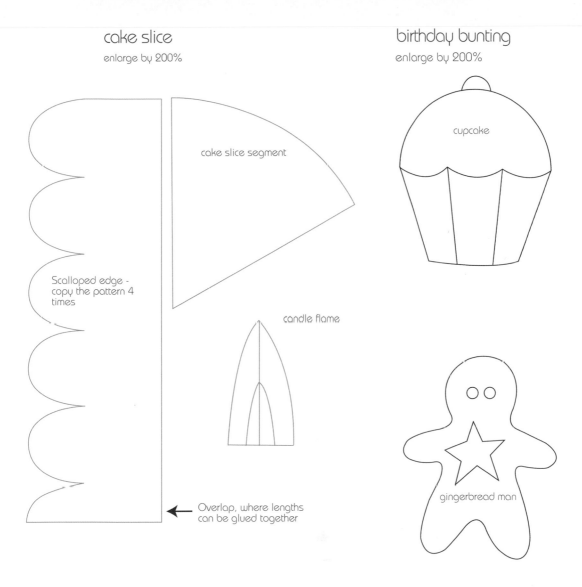

cake slice segment

cupcake

Scalloped edge -
copy the pattern 4
times

candle flame

Overlap, where lengths
can be glued together

gingerbread man

# designer credits

The publishers would like to thank the following designers who have allowed the reproduction of their designs in this book.

**Flower Felt Necklace**
Sally Southern

**Pretty Paper Earrings**
Margot Potter

**Button Bangle**
Jill Gorski

**Moody Blues**
Sally Southern

**Magic Mitten Gloves**
Claire Crompton

**Simple Socks**
Louise Butt

**Ballerina Slippers**
Louise Butt

**Fabric Frames**
Sally Southern

**iPod Sweater**
Julie Collings

**Dishy Delight**
Sally Southern

**Pucker-Up Purse**
Jenny Hill

**Birdie Album**
Jenn Docherty

**Retro Cards**
Sharon Bennett

**Cake Slice**
Marion Elliot

**Stuffed Chicks**
Julie Collings

**Neapolitan Soap Pops**
Debbie Chialtas

**Birthday Bunting**
Dorothy Wood

**Button Baby Dolls**
Jill Gorski

**Funky Flowers**
Julie Hickey

**Cupcake Bag**
Sally Southern

# index

Album, Birdie 50–53
appliqué 16, 78, 88,
   91–92, 93, 94

backstitch 43, 87, 88
bag charm 19
Bags
   Cupcake 78–81
   Jeans 16–19
Bangle, Button 14
blanket stitch 64, 88
Bunting, Birthday 70
Button Baby Dolls 72
buttonhole stitch 25, 70, 88
buttons 14, 22, 25, 30, 44,
   56, 72, 78, 80–81, 91

card 54, 58–59, 76–77,
   110–113
Cards, Retro 54
catch stitch 11, 70, 89
Chicks, Stuffed 62–65
crochet
   abbreviations 108
   edging 33
   hook sizes 108
   stitches 109

Earrings, Pretty Paper 12

fabric 18–19, 38–39, 44,
   64–65, 80–81, 85, 86–87
felt 8, 10–11, 14, 42–43,
   52–53, 70, 80–81
flowers, paper 74–77
Frames, Fabric 36–39
French knots 89

Gloves, Magic Mitten
   20–25

iPod Sweater 40–43

key ring 19
knitting
   abbreviations 96–97
   binding off 105
   casting on 98
   darning in ends 106
   decreasing stitches
   104–105
   gauge 96
   in the round 102
   increasing stitches 103
   mittens 106–107

sewing up 106
   stitches 99–101
knitting projects 22–25,
   28–29, 32–33, 48–49

Necklace, Felt Flower 8–11
needle felting projects
   42–43, 52–53
needles
   felting 42, 52–53
   knitting 22–25, 28–29,
     32–33, 48–49, 84,
     96, 97, 98–107
   sewing 14, 18, 64–65,
     84, 87–89, 90, 91,
     93–95

owlet, stuffed 65

paper
   curling 111–112
   rolling 112
papercraft projects 12, 54,
   58–59, 76–77
patterns, preparing 85
pinning 85, 94
Purse, Pucker-Up 46–49

ring, felt 11
running stitch 10, 19, 39,
   70, 80–81, 89, 94

seams 89, 94–95, 106–107
sequins 8, 10, 30, 36,
   38–39, 70, 90
sewing
   by hand 87–89
   machine 93–95
   stitches 88–89, 94–95
sewing projects 18–19,
   38–39, 44, 64–65, 70,
   80–81
Slippers, Ballerina 30–33
slipstitch 49, 89
soap making 66–69
Socks, Simple 26–29
straight stitch 94

tacking/basting 94, 95
templates 85, 92, 114–19
trinket dish 44

yo-yos 36, 39

zigzag stitch 94